SMOKING AND HEALTH

Summary and Report of
The Royal College of Physicians of London
on Smoking
in relation to
Cancer of the Lung
and
Other Diseases

PITMAN PUBLISHING CORPORATION

NEW YORK   TORONTO   LONDON

First published in Great Britain by Pitman Medical Publishing Co. Ltd.
© 1962 by The Royal College of Physicians of London
Copyright © 1962 by Pitman Publishing Corporation
2 West 45 Street, New York 36, N Y.

Library of Congress Catalogue Card Number 62-15794

SUMMARY

Introduction

Several serious diseases, in particular lung cancer, affect smokers more often than non-smokers. Cigarette smokers have the greatest risk of dying from these diseases, and the risk is greater for the heavier smokers. The many deaths caused by these diseases present a challenge to medicine, in so far as they are due to smoking they should be preventable. This report is intended to give to doctors and others evidence on the hazards of smoking so that they may decide what should be done (*paras. 1-3*).

History of Smoking

After its introduction to Europe in the 16th century, tobacco smoking, mostly in pipes, rapidly became popular. It has always had its advocates and opponents, but only recently has scientific study produced valid evidence of its ill-effects upon health. Cigarettes have largely replaced other forms of smoking in the past seventy years, during which time tobacco consumption has steadily increased. It is still increasing. Women hardly ever smoked before 1920: since then they have smoked steadily increasing numbers of cigarettes (*Figure 1, p. 3*) (*paras. 5-6*).

Present Smoking Habits

Three-quarters of the men and half of the women in Britain smoke. Men smoke more heavily than women. Smoking is now widespread among schoolchildren, especially boys. (*Figures 2 and 3, pp. 5 and 7*) (*paras. 7-8*). Many doctors have given up smoking since the dangers of the habit have become apparent: only half of them now smoke and less than a third smoke cigarettes (*Figures 4 and 5, pp. 9 and 11*) (*paras. 9 and 11*).

Advertising of Tobacco. There has been a steep increase in expenditure on advertisements of tobacco goods recently. Over 11 million pounds was spent on such advertisements in 1960 (*Table 1, p. 6; Figure 6, p. 13*). The increase has mostly been devoted to advertising cigarettes and many recent advertisements have been aimed at young people. It cannot, however, be assumed that advertisements are responsible for the continuing increase in tobacco consumption today (*paras. 10-11*).

Chemistry and Pharmacology of Tobacco Smoke

Tobacco smoke is complex in composition. Its most important components are: nicotine which acts on the heart, blood vessels, digestive tract, kidneys and nervous system; minute amounts of various substances which can produce cancer; and irritants which chiefly affect the bronchial tubes. The amounts of carbon monoxide and arsenic in the smoke are probably too small to be harmful (*paras. 12-22*).

Smoking and Cancer of the Lung

There has been a great increase in deaths from this disease in many countries during the past 45 years (*Figure 7, p. 15*). Some of this increase may be due to better diagnosis, but much of it is due to a real increase in incidence. Men are much more often affected than women. (*Table II, p. 14*) (*paras. 23-24,*)

Surveys. Many comparisons have been made in different countries between the smoking habits of patients with lung cancer and those of patients of the same age and sex with other diseases. All have shown that more lung cancer patients are smokers, and more of them heavy smokers than are the controls. The association between smoking and lung cancer has been confirmed by prospective studies in which the smoking habits of large numbers of men have been recorded and their deaths from various diseases observed subsequently. All these studies have shown that death rates from lung cancer increase steeply with increasing consumption of cigarettes. Heavy cigarette smokers may have thirty times the death rate of non-smokers. (*Figure 8, p. 17*). They have also shown that cigarette smokers are much more affected than pipe or cigar smokers (*Figure 9, p, 19*) and that those who had given up smoking at the start of the surveys had lower death rates than those who had continued to smoke (*Figure 10, p. 21*). Various criticisms, based on possible errors of selection and of diagnosis, which might have caused a spurious association between smoking and lung cancer in these studies, are discussed (*paras. 25-29*).

Pathology of Smokers' Lungs. Of three types of lung cancer, only the two commoner types are associated with smoking. The lungs of smokers without cancer show changes of chronic irritation, of the sort which might precede cancer, more often than the lungs of non-smokers (*paras. 30-31*).

Interpretation of the Evidence. The association of lung cancer with cigarette smoking is generally agreed to be true but various possible explanations of this association other than that of cause and effect have to be considered These are (*para. 32*).:—

(i) that people who are going to get lung cancer have an increased desire to smoke throughout their adult lives:

(ii) that smoking produces cancer only in the lungs of people who are in any case going to get cancer somewhere in the body, so that smoking determines only the site of the cancer:

(iii) that lung cancer affects people who would have died of tuberculosis in former times but have now survived with lungs susceptible to cancer:

(iv) that smokers inherit their desire to smoke and with it inherit a susceptibility to some other undiscovered agent that causes lung cancer:

(v) that smokers are by their nature more liable to many diseases, including lung cancer, than the "self-protective" minority of non-smokers:

(vi) that smokers tend to drink more alcohol than non-smokers so that drinking and not smoking may cause lung cancer:

(vii) that motor car exhausts, or—

(viii) that generalised air pollution may render the lungs of smokers more liable to cancer.

None of these explanations fits all the facts as well as the obvious one that smoking is a cause of lung cancer. There are other causes, including air pollution and substances which may be met in a few occupations, but none of them is of such general importance as smoking (*para. 33*).

There are a few facts which may be considered to conflict with this conclusion namely:—

   (i) that lung cancer occurs in only a minority of smokers:

   (ii) that death rates from this disease are lower in some countries than would be expected from their cigarette consumption:

   (iii) that there is some conflicting evidence on the effects of inhalation of smoke:

   (iv) that no animal has yet been given lung cancer by exposure to cigarette smoke.

Conclusion. These facts are discussed (*paras. 33-40*) and none of them is found to contradict the conclusion that cigarette smoking is an important cause of lung cancer. If the habit ceased, the number of deaths caused by this disease should fall steeply in the course of time (*para. 41*).

Smoking and Other Lung Diseases

Chronic bronchitis is a common and distressing disease in Britain and causes many deaths, especially in middle aged and elderly men. Smokers, particularly cigarette smokers, are much more often affected than non-smokers (*Figure 11, p. 29*). Other agents, of which generalised air pollution is the most important, are involved and it may be that damage done to the bronchial tubes by cigarette smoke makes them more susceptible to these other agents. Many men and women who are now disabled by chronic bronchitis might have remained well had they not smoked (*paras. 42-50*).

Smoking may possibly contribute to the development of pulmonary tuberculosis, especially in the middle-aged and elderly (*paras. 51-52*).

Smoking and Diseases of the Heart and Blood Vessels

Coronary heart disease is a more frequent cause of death in smokers, particularly cigarette smokers, than in non-smokers, although the latter are also commonly affected (*Table III, p. 34*). Those who give up smoking have a reduced death rate (*Figure 12, p. 33*). Many other factors, such as mental strain, sedentary occupation and diet, may explain some of the association of this disease with smoking, but cigarette smoking probably plays a significant part in rendering men in early middle age more liable to its serious effects. (*paras. 53-57*).

Smoking appears to play a part in causing other arterial diseases but not high blood pressure (*paras. 58-59*).

Smoking and Gastro-intestinal Diseases

Smoking affects the movements and secretion of the gut in many ways and may cause symptoms such as nausea and discomfort. It depresses appetite and may reduce weight. It does not appear to cause gastric or duodenal ulcers but interferes with their healing (*paras. 60-65*).

Cancers of the mouth, throat and gullet occur more frequently in smokers than in non-smokers (*para. 66*).

Smoking and Other Conditions

Several relatively uncommon diseases occur more often in smokers than non-smokers (*paras. 67-69*). Smokers may be more liable to accidents than non-smokers (*para. 70*). Women who smoke tend to have babies that are underweight (*para. 71*). Smoking may impair athletic performance (*para. 72*).

The Psychological Aspect of Smoking

Very little is known about why people smoke. Children tend to follow their parents' smoking habits. Intelligent children smoke less than duller children. Adults claim that smoking gives a sense of relaxation, helps them to concentrate and gives them relief when they are anxious, but these claims are difficult to test. Psychologists have suggested various unconscious motives for smoking (*paras. 73-78*).

Smokers tend to be more restless, less dependable and more neurotic than non-smokers. Cigarette smokers are more extraverted than non-smokers, pipe smokers are more introverted. That the tendency to smoke may be partly inborn is shown by studies of the smoking habits of twins (*para. 79*).

Smokers may be addicted to nicotine. They may wish to stop smoking for a variety of reasons, chiefly because of expense or fear of ill health. It appears that social factors play a bigger part in determining smoking habits than internal drives or needs (*paras. 80-82*).

Conclusions

The benefits of smoking are almost entirely psychological and social. It may help some people to avoid obesity. There is no reason to suppose that smoking prevents neurosis (*paras. 83-85*).

Cigarette smoking is a cause of lung cancer, and bronchitis and probably contributes to the development of coronary heart disease and various other less common diseases. It delays healing of gastric and duodenal ulcers (*paras. 86-89*).

The risks of smoking to the individual are calculated from death rates in relation to smoking habits among British doctors (*Table IV, p. 44*). The chance of dying in the next ten years for a man aged 35 who is a heavy cigarette smoker is 1 in 23 whereas the risk for a non-smoker is only 1 in 90. Only 15 per cent (one in six) of men of this age who are non-smokers but 33 per cent (one in three) of heavy smokers will die before the age of 65. Not all this difference in expectation of life is attributable to smoking (*paras. 90-91*).

The number of deaths caused by diseases associated with smoking is large (*Table V, p. 47*) (*para. 92*).

The need for preventive measures. Reduction in general air pollution should reduce the risks of cigarette smoking; but it is necessary for the health of the people in Britain that any measures that are practicable and likely to produce beneficial changes in smoking habits shall be taken promptly (*paras. 93-95*).

Preventive Measures

Since it is not yet possible to identify those individuals who will be harmed by smoking, preventive measures must be generally applied (*para. 96*).

The harmful effects of cigarette smoking might be reduced by efficient filters, by using modified tobaccos, by leaving longer cigarette stubs or by changing from cigarette to pipe or cigar smoking (*paras. 97-102*).

General discouragement of smoking, particularly by young people, is necessary. More effort needs to be expended on discovering the most effective means of dissuading children from starting the smoking habit (*paras. 103-107*). There can be no doubt of our responsibility for protecting future generations from

S7

developing the dependence on cigarette smoking that is so widespread today.

Most adults have heard of the risks of cigarette smoking but remain unconvinced. Doctors, who see the consequences of the habit, have reduced their cigarette consumption. Some evidence of concern by the Government is needed to convince the public. The Government have so far only asked local health authorities to carry out health education in respect of smoking, but little seems to have been achieved. The Central Council for Health Education and Local Authorities spent less than £5,000 on anti-smoking education in 1956-60, while the Tobacco Manufacturers spent £38,000,000 on advertising their goods during this period (*paras. 108-111*).

Possible Action by the Government

Decisive steps should be taken by the Government to curb the present rising consumption of tobacco, and especially of cigarettes. This action could be taken along the following lines (*paras. 112-119*):—

   (i) more education of the public and especially school-children concerning the hazards of smoking:

  (ii) more effective restrictions on the sale of tobacco to children:

 (iii) restriction of tobacco advertising:

 (iv) wider restriction of smoking in public places:

  (v) an increase of tax on cigarettes, perhaps with adjustment of the tax on pipe and cigar tobaccos:

 (vi) informing purchasers of the tar and nicotine content of the smoke of cigarettes:

(vii) investigating the value of anti-smoking clinics to help those who find difficulty in giving up smoking.

Doctors and Their Patients

There are good medical grounds for advising patients with bronchitis, peptic ulcer or arterial diseases to stop smoking. Even a smoker's cough may be an indication that the habit should be given up. Doctors are better able to help their patients to stop smoking if they do not smoke themselves. They have a special responsibility for public education about the dangers of smoking (*paras. 120-121*).

SMOKING AND HEALTH

A Report of
The Royal College of Physicians of London
on Smoking
in relation to
Cancer of the Lung
and
Other Diseases

FOREWORD TO THE AMERICAN EDITION

Since 1725, the highly esteemed Royal College of Physicians has made pronouncements on questions of public health when they felt that action was required. In keeping with this tradition, they have now investigated the subject of smoking in relation to lung cancer and other diseases. In this volume, they review the evidence point by point which has led them to conclude that cigarette smoking is a serious hazard to health. The reader is asked to accept nothing on faith. Every statement is documented. Contrary opinions are presented fairly and evaluated on their merits.

Other authoritative bodies which have expressed similar conclusions include the British Ministry of Health, the British Medical Research Council, the National Cancer Institute of Canada, the International Union Against Cancer, the World Health Organization, and the Netherlands Ministry of Social Affairs and Public Health. In this country, the United States Public Health Service, the American Public Health Association, the Public Health Cancer Association, the American Heart Association, and the National Tuberculosis Association have all issued warnings to the public.

The American Cancer Society, which is particularly concerned about the rapid rise in lung cancer, conducted several of the studies described in this book and has contributed over $4,000,000 in support of lung cancer research. The board of directors of the American Cancer Society has stated that "many studies reported in recent years indicate beyond reasonable doubt that cigarette smoking is the major cause of the unprecedented increase in lung cancer."

The Royal College of Physicians has made a number of specific recommendations concerning action to be taken in Great Britain. The American Cancer Society is promoting the widespread dissemination of information (particularly to teenagers) on smoking in relation to cancer and is on record approving "action to require labeling of cigarette packages with tar and nicotine content."

I highly recommend this book to those who wish to hear the evidence from which they can draw their own conclusions concerning the effects of cigarette smoking.

E. Cuyler Hammond, Sc. D.
Director, Statistical Research Section
Medical Affairs Department, American Cancer Society

New York, March 1962

INTRODUCTION

1. Several serious illnesses, in particular lung cancer, affect smokers more often than non-smokers. Heavier smokers have a higher death rate than lighter smokers: those who continue to smoke have a higher death rate than those who stop: cigarette smokers have a higher death rate than smokers of pipes or cigars. There is no doubt of the truth of these statements; dispute continues only about their interpretation. While some maintain that the association between smoking and diseases is one of cause and effect, others believe that smoking habits and diseases may be separately related to some other common factors, such as inherited constitution or general air pollution, so that an association between smoking and any disease may not imply that the one causes the other. Diseases associated with smoking now cause so many deaths that they present one of the most challenging opportunities for preventive medicine today. Physicians therefore need to know the facts, consider what they mean, then decide what action they should take themselves, what advice they should give their patients and what policy they should advocate in the field of public health in relation to tobacco smoking.

2. It was for these reasons that the Royal College of Physicians decided on April 30th, 1959, to set up a Committee "to report on the question of smoking and atmospheric pollution in relation to carcinoma of the lung and other diseases". There is good historical precedent for the Royal College of Physicians pronouncing on a question of public health when action is required. An early example was the College's representation to the House of Commons in 1725 concerning the disastrous consequences of the rising consumption of cheap gin. This played an important part in initiating legislation which ultimately brought this abuse under control[31]. The College has always been concerned with important matters of public health.

3. The report which follows recounts the history of tobacco smoking in Britain, emphasises recent trends, reviews the evidence for and against the hypothesis that smoking causes various kinds of disease, discusses the psychological aspects of smoking and

1

makes recommendations as to the action which may be required in the light of present evidence. The important effects of atmospheric pollution will be the subject of a separate report. Although the effects of this hazard and of tobacco smoking may be inter-related, at least in the case of lung cancer and bronchitis, the preventive measures required in respect of air pollution are of a character so entirely different from those required in respect of smoking that the two hazards are best considered separately.

4. Since many detailed reviews of the effects of smoking are already available this report is confined to a full summary of the evidence and a discussion of its interpretation, without setting out every detail. The arguments are presented in a manner that should be comprehensible by interested laymen, as well as by doctors.

HISTORY OF SMOKING[143]

5. Tobacco smoking in pipes was first introduced to western civilisation by the Spanish explorers of America in the early 16th century. English explorers of the New World brought it to England and by 1590 sufficient quantities were being imported for the Queen to impose the first import duty of 2d. a pound. It is remarkable that tobacco should have attained such rapid popularity among people quite unaccustomed to it, particularly since the early tobaccos produced rank smoke with a much higher nicotine content than modern smokers would relish. Tobacco was recommended for its medicinal value by Jean Nicot, French Ambassador to Lisbon, after whom nicotine was named but it soon became the subject of acute controversy. It was both praised as a prophylactic against many ills and a restorative and condemned as a noxious vice, in particular by James I in his famous "Counterblaste to Tobacco". This controversy has continued almost unabated ever since but, until recently, with no valid evidence on either side.

6. Throughout the 17th century tobacco consumption in England rose steadily, mostly in the form of pipe smoking, but tobacco was also chewed and snuffed. Towards the end of the century smoking was largely replaced in fashionable circles by snuff-taking but the mass of the people continued to smoke pipes and tobacco consumption continued to rise. Cigars were introduced at the beginning of the 19th century but were never as popular in England as on the continent. Cigarettes were first made in Spain in the mid-17th century. The habit of smoking them appears to have been introduced into England by troops returning from the Crimean War. The production of milder tobaccos in Virginia and the development of the briar pipe in 1860, together with increasing prosperity, resulted in a further steady rise of tobacco consumption throughout the 19th century, but cigarettes only

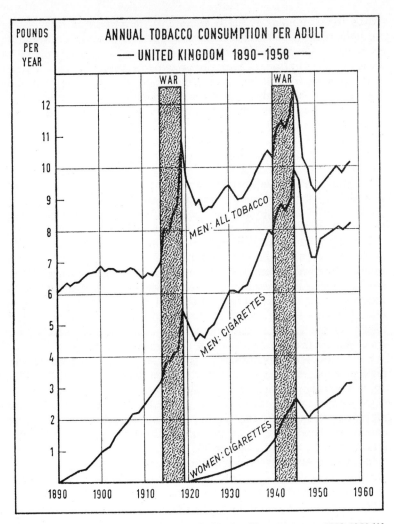

FIGURE 1   TOBACCO CONSUMPTION IN THE UNITED KINGDOM FROM 1890-1958.[189]

These figures give the annual consumption of tobacco in pounds per adult (age 16 and over). Ten pounds of tobacco are equivalent to about 4500 cigarettes which, if consumed in one year, implies smoking an average of about 12 cigarettes per day.

The steady trend of increasing cigarette consumption by men was interrupted by sharp peaks of increases during both wars. Cigarette consumption by men has increased much more rapidly than their total consumption so that there has been a steady decrease in other forms of smoking. Women hardly smoked at all until after the first War, and although they have increased their consumption of cigarettes faster than men in the last twenty years, they still smoke far less than men.

3

began to be popular at the beginning of the present century. Since then cigarettes have steadily tended to replace other forms of smoking in Britain. During both World Wars there were high peaks of tobacco consumption. In both post-war periods there was a sharp fall in consumption followed by a steady rise. Women rarely smoked before 1920. Since then cigarette consumption by women has increased steadily apart from a temporary fall between 1945 and 1948 (Figure 1, p. 3).

PRESENT SMOKING HABITS

7. Most smokers adopt the habit during adolescence, but recent national surveys published by the Tobacco Manufacturers' Standing Committee[189] and several independent surveys of schoolchildren ranging from the Isle of Wight to Lancashire[18, 28, 107, 186] have shown that while there are considerable variations from one kind of school to another (see paragraph 74) in general 11% to 15% of boys, not infrequently with parental consent or even encouragement, are already smoking small numbers of cigarettes by the age of 10. During schooldays there is a steady recruitment to smoking with a sharp rise at the school leaving age of 15, till at the age of 19 adult habits are established (Figure 2.) Girls smoke less often but by the age of 15 about 15% and by the age of 20, about 40% smoke regularly.

8. During adult life, nearly 75% of men and 50% of women are regular smokers. Men who smoke cigarettes consume an average of 19 and women 11 cigarettes a day. The percentage distribution of cigarette consumption (Figure 3, p. 7) shows that there are many more heavy smokers and fewer light smokers among men than among women. Pipe smoking is confined to men and is predominantly found in those over the age of 60.

9. The smoking habits of male doctors contrast notably with those of other men. A questionnaire, sent in 1961 to a random sample of nearly 500 male doctors qualified for ten years or more, and answered by 92%, showed that half the doctors are now non-smokers compared with only about a quarter (24%) of other men of the same ages, and that less than a third of the doctors smoke only cigarettes compared with more than a half of all men (54%) (Figure 4, p. 9)[58]. Some indication that this contrast is of recent origin is given by comparing the replies to the 1961 questionnaires with replies given by those doctors in this sample who also replied to a similar questionnaire 10 years previously[57]. Between 1951 and 1961, one in every three smokers gave up smoking while only one in twelve non-smokers or ex-smokers started. Altogether the proportion of non-smokers increased from 40% to 56% and the proportion of cigarette smokers decreased from

4

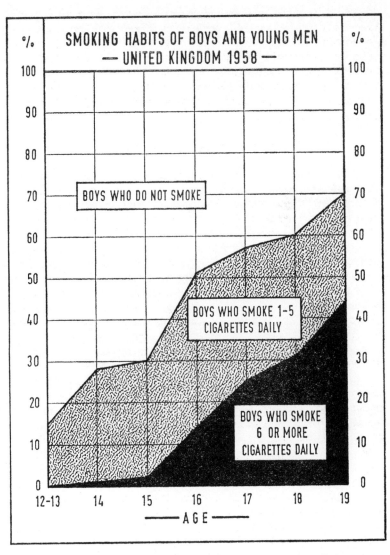

FIGURE 2 THE ONSET OF SMOKING IN BOYS AND YOUNG MEN

Although light smoking is quite common by the age of 15, serious smoking (of 6 or more cigarettes daily) only begins to be frequent after leaving school. Thereafter its frequency rapidly increases. (Figures provided by the Tobacco Manufacturers' Standing Committee).

5

38% to 23%* (Figure 5, p. 11). Similar changes have been reported in New England, U.S.A.[180] That these changes are not simply those which may be expected to take place with increasing age is suggested by the finding that in doctors of the same ages there were fewer cigarette smokers and more non-smokers in 1961 than in 1951. In contrast to this trend, the consumption of cigarettes per head of the general population has risen steadily and is still rising (Figure 1, p. 3).

Advertisement of Tobacco Goods

10. There have been impressive increases in expenditure on the advertising of tobacco goods in recent years. Figures supplied by the

TABLE I

ESTIMATED ANNUAL EXPENDITURE IN THE UNITED KINGDOM ON ADVERTISING CIGARETTES, TOBACCO AND SMOKERS' REQUISITES.
(£'000 p.a.)

YEAR	MEDIUM					APPROX TOTAL £ million
	Press	T.V.	Poster[1]	Cinema[1]	Signs[1, 2]	
1955	1,891	38[3]	475	245	900	3·7
1956	2,303	398	550	275	925	4·5
1957	2,734	1,341	800	435	1,000	6·5
1958	2,879	2,054	950	375	1,100	7·5
1959	2,822	2,990	950	350	1,100	8·2
1960	4,007	4,558	850	300	1,200	11·0

[1] Approximate.   [2] Outdoor signs and point of sale.
[3] Sept.-Dec., and only from London and home counties.
No estimates are available for other forms, e.g. gifts.
Total expenditure on all advertising is estimated at £277 million in 1955 and £453 million in 1960.

Tobacco Advisory Committee and the Economist Intelligence Unit are given in Table I and Figure 6, p. 13. During a period (1955-60-when total expenditure on advertising has not quite doubled, expendi) ture on tobacco advertising has increased threefold. The total expenditure in 1960 was approximately £11,000,000. Much of this increased expenditure has been devoted to establishing loyalty to particular brands of cigarettes and no advertisements have specifically encouraged heavier smoking. There is, however, no evidence of any attempt to encourage pipe tobacco and cigars in preference to cigarettes. Indeed the increase has been much greater for cigarettes, the smoking of

* This sample of doctors contains a greater proportion of non-smokers and a smaller proportion of cigarette smokers than either the total sample of doctors who answered the questionnaire in 1951 or the total sample taken in 1961. The smokers in 1951 who are included in this sample may, however, be regarded as representative of all doctors who smoked then, so that the changes in smoking habits of these doctors that have occurred since 1951 may be taken to indicate the changes that have occurred in the smoking habits of all doctors during the past 10 years.

CIGARETTE CONSUMPTION OF MEN & WOMEN WHO SMOKE
— UNITED KINGDOM. 1958 —

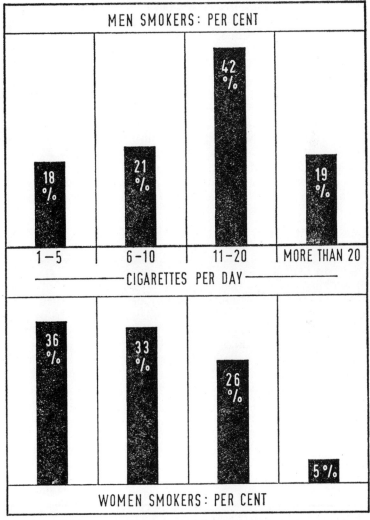

FIGURE 3. THE CONTRAST BETWEEN CIGARETTE SMOKING BY MEN AND WOMEN.

The majority of men who smoke consume more than 10 cigarettes daily and one in five of them smoke more than 20 daily. The majority of women who smoke, on the other hand, consume ten or less cigarettes daily and only 1 in 20 of them smoke more than 20 cigarettes daily.

7

which, as will be described later, is more closely associated with disease and premature death than is pipe or cigar smoking. In recent years there has been a notable shift in the type and aims of cigarette advertising. Advertisements with romantic allusions give the appearance of being addressed increasingly to young people who may not yet be addicted to the habit or attached to any particular brand.

11. It cannot be assumed that the increase in advertising is the only or even the main reason for rising tobacco consumption. Figures, unfortunately, are available for only one country in which there is no direct advertising of tobacco: in Czechoslovakia[182] the annual consumption of cigarettes per inhabitant over the age of 15 rose by 14% (from 3·6 to 4·1 pounds) between 1953 and 1958. During the same period in the United Kingdom, the annual consumption of cigarettes per adult also rose by 14% (from 5 to 5·7 pounds). It would be unwise, however, to conclude from this comparison that advertising is without effect on cigarette consumption; for the factors that determine this are certainly complex and a solitary comparison between two countries which differ in so many ways may be misleading.*

THE CHEMISTRY AND PHARMACOLOGY OF SMOKING

12. Tobacco smoke is a mixture of gases and minute droplets ranging in diameter from 10 to 40 millionths of an inch (0·3 to 1·0 microns)[111, 119]. A varying proportion, about 50%, of inhaled smoke is retained in the lungs. Some droplets are deposited directly on the walls of the bronchial tubes, others are taken up by motile cells, chiefly in the air sacs. Many of these cells migrate into the bronchial tubes and then pass upwards over their lining membrane.

13. Tobacco smoke is extremely complex in composition; some 300 compounds having been identified in it[12, 110]. The composition varies with the type of tobacco, the way in which it has been cured and the way it is smoked, but little is known of the medical importance of these variations. Cigarettes, especially when smoked fast, burn at a higher temperature than pipes and cigars[118, 134]. The main stream smoke of cigarettes is faintly acid, that of pipes may be acid or alkaline, while cigar smoke is faintly alkaline[34, 37, 134, 165]. Alkaline smoke tends to be more irritating and thus less readily inhaled[165]. The paper of cigarettes provides an insignificant contribution to the smoke[39]. The compounds of tobacco smoke of chief medical interest are:—

14. **Nicotine.** The amount of nicotine that can be recovered from the main-stream smoke of one cigarette varies from 1 to 3 milligrams[116].

* A memorandum on the advertising of tobacco goods submitted by the Tobacco Advisory Committee is printed in Appendix 1.

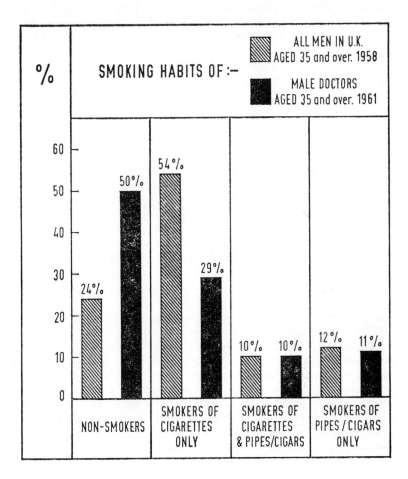

FIGURE 4 THE CONTRAST BETWEEN SMOKING HABITS OF MALE DOCTORS AND OTHER MEN IN THE U.K.

Twice as many doctors as other men are non-smokers. This difference is almost wholly due to differences in the number who smoke cigarettes. These differences between doctors and other men have largely come about in recent years since doctors have become aware of the evidence of the harmful effects of cigarette smoking (see Figure 5). The figures for doctors are based upon a sample survey of all doctors aged 35 and over carried out by Hill and Doll in 1961[58]. Those for the general population of men of this age are taken from Research Paper No. 1 of the Tobacco Manufacturers' Standing Committee[189].

Of this, smokers who inhale may absorb as much as 90% and those who do not, as little as 10%[86, 123]. The chief effects of such a dose of nicotine are on the heart and blood vessels, the digestive tract and the kidneys.

15. Nicotine causes constriction of the superficial vessels in the limbs, raises the blood pressure and augments the pulse rate and output of the heart by both direct and indirect effects[23, 171, 172]. There is little evidence in normal subjects of any significant effect upon the blood flow in the coronary arteries which nourish the heart[8,] but changes in the electrocardiogram suggest that the flow may be reduced by nicotine in patients with coronary artery disease[125, 142, 171]. There is considerable individual variation in these reactions.

16. In the digestive tract[10, 156] the effects are also complex and variable. The nausea and vomiting that often follow the first attempt to smoke are probably indirect results of a stimulant effect on the central nervous system. Secretion of saliva and movement of the gut are at first stimulated and then depressed.

17. Secretion of urine is reduced in volume by the release of "anti-diuretic hormone" from the pituitary gland and perhaps also by the secretion of adrenaline[24].

18. Burn[22] has recently suggested that there may be a pharmacological basis for the reputed stimulating action of nicotine on the brain.

19. **Carcinogenic substances.** Some sixteen different substances capable of initiating cancer in experimental animals have hitherto been identified in tobacco smoke,[40 63, 114, 137,] most of them in infinitesimal amounts. The experimental production of cancer in animals by substances condensed from tobacco smoke is considered later in this report (paragraphs 37-39).

20. **Irritants.** The irritant effect of tobacco smoke upon mucous membranes is probably due to a variety of substances among which ammonia, volatile acids, aldehydes, phenols and ketones may all play a part. This effect is probably of chief importance in the respiratory tract, where tobacco smoke stimulates the secretion of mucus and delays its removal by slowing the action of the ciliated lining of the bronchial tubes[7, 44, 100].*

21. **Carbon monoxide** is found in tobacco smoke, but even in heavy smokers the percentage of haemoglobin† combined with carbon monoxide is seldom as much as 5%, though it may rise to just over 10% after a series of cigarettes have been smoked[124]. This is not enough to have clinical effects in normal circumstances.

* The bronchial tubes are lined with a membrane equipped with fine hair-like processes called cilia which beat in waves and this beating keeps the film of mucus which lies on the surface moving steadily upwards. This moving film of mucus is the means by which the lung is freed from nearly all the dust and germs which are inhaled.
† The red pigment that carries oxygen in the blood.

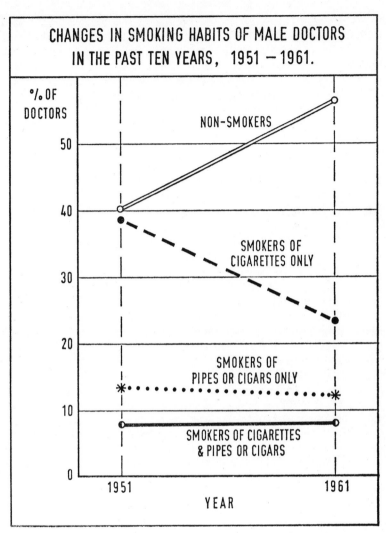

FIGURE 5 CHANGES IN THE SMOKING HABITS OF MALE DOCTORS IN THE PAST 10 YEARS[58]

This figure illustrates changes in the last ten years in the smoking habits of those doctors who replied to questionnaires in 1951 and 1961. Although there were rather more non-smokers and fewer cigarette smokers in this sample than among doctors as a whole, the changes that occurred during this period may be taken to represent the changes that have occurred generally among doctors. The proportion of non-smokers has risen and the proportion of cigarette smokers has fallen, while there has been little change in the proportion of those who smoke pipes and cigars with or without cigarettes. These changes have occurred since the dangers of cigarette smoking have become known. There has been no corresponding change in the smoking habits of the general population during the same period.

11

22. **Arsenic.** This is of interest because it is a carcinogen. It used to be present in tobacco smoke in very variable amounts, being derived from arsenical insecticides used in tobacco plantations. The use of these substances has declined[192] and the arsenic content of cigarettes is now infinitesimal. There has never been enough arsenic in tobacco for this to be likely to cause cancer by itself[42, 43, 50] but it might have had an adjuvant (or co-carcinogenic) action, whose significance cannot be dismissed.

SMOKING AND CANCER OF THE LUNG

Increasing Death rates from Lung Cancer

23. During the past 45 years lung cancer has changed from an infrequent to a major cause of death in many countries. This increase has been most serious in men and women in late middle age, when family and professional responsibilities are at their height. Table II, p. 14 shows the total number of deaths that have occurred in men and women between the ages of 45 and 64 since 1916; and Figure 7, p. 15 presents the age-standardised death rate for men in these age groups during the same period from cancer of the lung, other forms of cancer, tuberculosis of the lungs and bronchitis. While death rates from lung cancer have been increasing, those from other forms of cancer, and other respiratory diseases have been declining or, like bronchitis, remaining stationary.

24. The experience of chest physicians and surgeons in the past 30 years leaves no doubt in their minds that there has been a very large and real increase in incidence of lung cancer, though some pathologists consider that the disease used to be more common than mortality figures suggest and that much of the increase may be due to improved accuracy of diagnosis on death certificates[193]. If there has been no increase it is difficult to see why cancer of the lung alone among all cancers should have become so much more frequently diagnosed in so many countries, and the much faster rate of increase in men than in women (Table II, p. 14) cannot be due to improved diagnosis. There must have been a notable increase even though it may not be so great as mortality figures suggest. To account for this increase it is necessary to postulate some causative agent to which human lungs have been newly and increasingly exposed during the present century. Cigarette smoke is such an agent and there is now a great deal of evidence that it is an important cause of this disease.

Retrospective Surveys

25. At least 23 investigations in nine countries[47, 51] have shown by retrospective study that among sufferers from lung cancer there is a

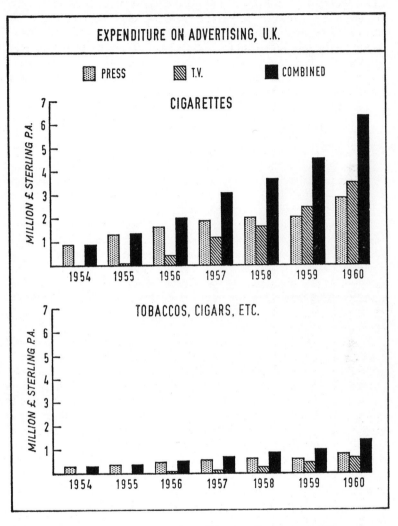

FIGURE 6 EXPENDITURE ON ADVERTISING TOBACCO GOODS IN THE PRESS AND ON
TELEVISION IN THE UNITED KINGDOM 1954-1960.

Three quarters of the money spent on tobacco goods pays for advertisements in the
press or on T.V. (Table I, p. 6). Much of the recent increase in expenditure has been
devoted to advertisements of cigarettes on television. Between 1954 and 1960 there
was a fivefold increase in advertising of cigarettes and only a threefold increase in
advertising pipe tobaccos and cigars.

TABLE II

AVERAGE ANNUAL NUMBERS OF DEATHS FROM VARIOUS CAUSES DURING FIVE YEAR PERIODS FROM 1916 TO 1959 IN MEN AND WOMEN AGED 45-64. ENGLAND AND WALES.

Disease Period	a Cancer of Lung (excluding mediastinum and trachea)		b Cancer other than Lung (excluding Hodgkin's Disease and Leukemia)		c Bronchitis (all forms) (including bronchiectasis)		d Tuberculosis of Lungs	
	Men	Women	Men	Women	Men	Women	Men	Women
1916-20	146	87	8,876	10,881	4,708*	3,504*	6,607	3,225
1921-25	255	121	10,325	12,034	3,804*	2,776*	5,689	2,635
1926-30	481	177	11,005	12,940	3,053*	1,947*	5,766	2,413
1931-35	1,158	324	11,185	13,718	2,339*	1,222*	5,488	2,134
1936-40	2,020	463	10,985	14,212	2,757*	1,086*	5,271	1,826
1941-45	3,090	566	10,458	14,284	5,644	1,954	5,146	1,522
1946-50	5,031	761	10,121	13,984	5,649	1,658	4,785	1,346
1951-55	7,348	980	10,027	13,831	6,238	1,614	2,862	742
1956-59†	9,108	1,202	10,265	14,119	6,437	1,526	1,484	345

a. 161·1 - 163; b. 140-200, 202, 203, 205; c. 500-502; 526; d. 001-008.
Current International Statistical Classification:
† 1960 figures not available.

* Figures not comparable with figures for later years because of changes in allocation of certified causes of death.

Figures kindly supplied by Dr. R. A. M. Case of the Chester Beatty Research Institute.

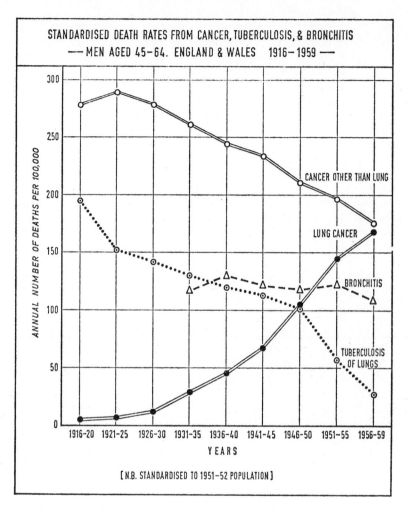

FIGURE 7 DEATH RATES FROM LUNG CANCER, OTHER FORMS OF CANCER, TUBER-
CULOSIS OF THE LUNGS AND BRONCHITIS IN MEN AGED 45-64 FROM 1916 TO 1959.

The increasing death rate from lung cancer over this period is most striking.
The decline in deaths from other forms of cancer has occurred chiefly in respect
of cancer of the liver, tongue, oesophagus and rectum. The sharp decline in
tuberculous mortality in the last decade is largely attributable to modern treatment.
Bronchitis mortality rates before 1931 were much higher than subsequently, but,
because of changes in the practice of death registration, the earlier figures are
not comparable to subsequent ones and have been omitted. Since 1931 bronchitis
death rates in middle aged men have changed very little.

15

higher proportion of heavy smokers and a lower proportion of light smokers or non-smokers than in comparable control groups. Not only have these studies all shown the same association, but among those dealing with larger numbers it is quantitatively similar, even though the investigations have been made in different countries.

26. The methods of these investigations have varied but in essence the answers to questions about smoking habits given by patients with lung cancer were compared with those given by individuals, usually patients in the same hospital, without lung cancer. Such methods are open to criticism because of several possible ways in which bias might have been introduced in spite of precautions which were taken. In one investigation, that of Doll and Hill[54, 55], the criticism that the amount smoked by cancer patients might have been over-estimated because the patient or the interviewer suspected the diagnosis (although interviewers were, in fact, not informed of the diagnosis) was met by the findings in a small group in whom lung cancer had been wrongly diagnosed. Patients in this group were at the time of the interview thought to be suffering from lung cancer, but subsequent investigation showed them to be suffering from some other disease: their smoking habits fell into line exactly with those of the control group. Another criticism was that the control group, which was usually composed of other patients in the same hospitals as the lung cancer patients, might not have represented a fair sample in respect of the smoking habits of the population from which the patients came. But comparison of the smoking habits of the hospital control group who lived in the Greater London area with those of the general population of the same area, showed that the hospital control group actually smoked more. This was to be expected in view of the association of smoking with several other diseases, and would actually lead to underestimation of the effect of smoking in predisposing to lung cancer in these retrospective studies.

Prospective Surveys

27. The results of retrospective studies have been fully confirmed by prospective studies in which, first, the smoking habits of a defined population group have been ascertained, and then the causes of death during several years' observation have been recorded. Four independent groups in three countries have conducted investigations of this sort[16, 56, 57, 62, 94]. They all show a steady increase in numbers of deaths from lung cancer with increasing cigarette consumption, and are in close quantitative agreement not only with each other but also with most of the retrospective studies. The results of the first three of these investigations are summarised in Figure 8. The rather higher mortality found in the British study compared with the American

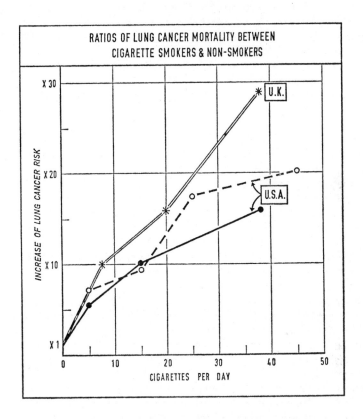

FIGURE 8   THE RELATIONSHIP BETWEEN NUMBERS OF CIGARETTES SMOKED PER DAY
AND LUNG CANCER DEATH RATES IN THREE PROSPECTIVE STUDIES.

The figure shows how much the risk of getting lung cancer is multiplied in those who smoke various numbers of cigarettes per day compared with the risk of non-smokers. The first horizontal line in the figure indicates ten times the risk of non-smokers, and so on.

The figures are derived from:—

Doll and Hill's study of British doctors aged 35 and over[57] (════*════).
Hammond and Horn's study of American men aged 50-69[94] (─ ─ ○ ─ ─).
Dorn's study of American ex-service men aged 30 and over[62] (━━━●━━━).

The similarity of the steady increase in lung cancer risk with increasing cigarette smoking found by these three independent studies is impressive. The higher British rates may be due to the British habit of smoking cigarettes to a shorter stub length than the Americans and to the greater exposure of British men to air polluted by domestic and industrial smoke.

studies, may be explained partly by the observation that the British smoke more of each cigarette than do the Americans, thus receiving a larger dose of smoke and losing the filtration effect of a long stub[59, 91] (see paras. 97 and 101), and partly, perhaps, by the greater exposure of the British to air polluted by chimney smoke[88]. These investigations in which estimates of relative risks for different forms of smoking were possible have all shown that pipe smokers incur a considerably smaller risk than cigarette smokers. The American investigations have also shown that the risk in those who smoke only cigars is even smaller (Figure 9) and may be no greater than that for non-smokers.

28. An important finding in all of these prospective investigations has been that the risk among those who have given up smoking for several years is less than among those who continue to smoke (Figure 10, p. 21).

29. The possibility of continuing observation of a selected population in a prospective study is particularly valuable since it provides an answer to the criticism that even in a prospective study initial selection bias may affect the results. The subjects in such a study are selected by the fact that they have replied to a questionnaire or have been chosen for interview, and bias might be introduced by inclusion of more or fewer smokers than non-smokers who are in ill health at the beginning of the observation period. In all these studies, however, the association between deaths from lung cancer and smoking was more evident in the later than in the earlier part of the observation period, which is the reverse of the trend that would be expected if the association was even in part due to initial selection bias. Another possible criticism of these prospective studies concerned accuracy of diagnosis, since in three studies the certified cause of death was accepted. Bias might be introduced, for example, if there were a special tendency for lung cancer to be diagnosed as the cause of death in heavy smokers. But the total death rate was found to increase with the amount smoked, the excess deaths among smokers being attributable principally to disease of the cardiovascular system, especially coronary thrombosis, and to certain respiratory diseases as well as to lung cancer. Hence if some of the deaths among smokers were being attributed falsely to lung cancer, the effect of smoking in increasing mortality from other diseases was underestimated. In the investigation of Doll and Hill and of Hammond and Horn, moreover, the association with smoking was actually greater for those cases of lung cancer in which the diagnosis had been established by the most certain method, i.e. by microscopic examination of diseased tissue, than for those in which it was dependent on clinical evidence alone.*

* For further discussion of the validity of the evidence provided by these surveys see references 13, 14, 41, 47, 51, 53, 128, 163.

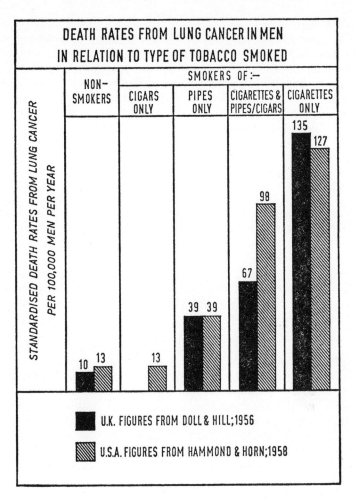

FIGURE 9 DEATH RATES FROM LUNG CANCER IN MEN ACCORDING TO THE TYPE OF TOBACCO SMOKED.

These figures are taken from the prospective study of British doctors aged 35 and over by Doll and Hill (Doll[53]) and of American men aged 50-69 by Hammond and Horn.[94] Only in the U.S.A. were there enough pure cigar smokers to estimate their death rate which was the same as for non-smokers. Pipe smokers had three times, smokers of cigarettes with pipes or cigars five to eight times and pure cigarette smokers about ten times the mortality of non-smokers. The similarity of the rates in both studies is impressive. The differences between cigarette smokers and other tobacco smokers may be due to the greater tendency of cigarette smokers to inhale the smoke (see para. 89).

Pathology

30. There are three principal pathological types of lung cancer, and precision in microscopical diagnosis shows that smoking is associated specifically with two of these. When Kreyberg in Norway made an independent classification of pathological sections from British cases investigated by Doll and Hill without knowing the smoking habits of the subjects, he found a close relationship between the daily amount smoked and the development of cancers described as squamous† and undifferentiated (which are now the commonest pathological types) but little or none with the less common cancers described as adeno-carcinomas†[60].

31. Several studies of non-cancerous changes in the bronchial epithelium in relation to smoking history have been published. Auerbach and his colleagues in New Jersey[5, 6] studied nearly 30,000 sections from the bronchi of 83 men who died of causes other than lung cancer, and 34 men who had died of lung cancer, all of whose smoking histories were known. There was a quantitative relationship between cigarette consumption and the frequency of microscopic changes suggesting chronic irritation. Such changes are possible precursors of some types of cancer and were most frequent in the men with lung cancer. Similar findings have been reported by other pathologists[30, 106, 173].

Interpretation of the Evidence

32. Various independent authoritative bodies* have been set up to examine the evidence of the relationship between cancer of the lung and smoking and have all agreed that it is established. The most obvious explanation of this association is that it is causal. There are, however, other possible explanations which must be considered.

(i) That many years before lung cancer becomes manifest some early process in its development may produce the desire to smoke. This hypothetical process must be postulated to begin to act as long as 40 to 50 years before the onset of clinical disease, to produce a desire to smoke a number of cigarettes daily in proportion to its liability to mature into cancer, to have become suddenly more prevalent within the past few decades, and to cause a desire for cigarettes rather than pipes or cigars. These postulates appear highly improbable.

(ii) That smoking may not cause cancer but only determine the site

† In squamous cancers the cells bear some resemblance to those found in the skin. In adeno-carcinoma the cells retain the appearance of those in glands.
* British Ministry of Health[146], British Medical Research Council[145], National Cancer Institute of Canada[152], Netherlands Ministry of Social Affairs and Public Health[153], U.S. Study Group of Smoking and Health 1957, U.S. Public Health Service[25, 191], World Health Organization[196].

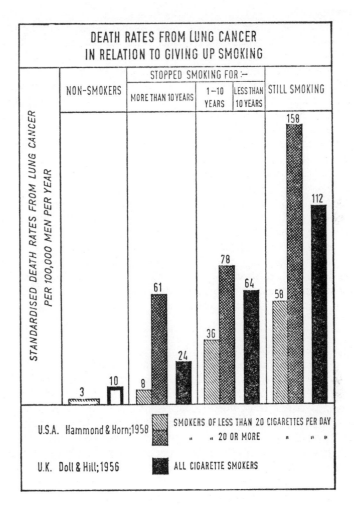

FIGURE 10 THE EFFECT OF GIVING UP SMOKING ON DEATH RATES FROM LUNG CANCER.

In this figure the death rates given for American men relate only to cases in which the diagnosis was established microscopically, so that these rates are lower than those illustrated from the same source in Figure 9, p. 19. The British figures are from Doll[53]. Only in the American study were heavier and lighter smokers separated. There was a similar, much reduced death rate in those who had given up smoking, especially if the period without smoking had been for more than ten years before the beginning of the study; but the heavier smokers who had given up smoking retained a higher mortality than the lighter smokers who continued to smoke.

at which it appears in subjects prone to cancer for some other reason. This possibility is disproved by the fact that other forms of cancer are not less common among smokers than among non-smokers[57].

(iii) That the rising death rate from lung cancer may be a consequence of the falling death rate from tuberculosis[15, 98]. "In relation to tuberculosis . . . persons whose constitutional make-up render them prone to a breakdown of the pulmonary system formerly died in early life of tuberculosis . . . There has been, so to speak, a survival of the unfit respiratory systems"[15]. There is little evidence to support this hypothesis, which also fails to account for the association of lung cancer with smoking. No one has shown that susceptibility to tuberculosis and lung cancer are related, and it will be seen in Table II, p. 14 that while tuberculosis mortality has fallen proportionately faster in women than in men the reverse is true of the increase of lung cancer.

(iv) That some factor may be independently associated with both lung cancer and cigarette smoking. The only factor seriously proposed is heredity, the suggestion being made, in particular by Fisher[73, 74], that subjects with a hereditary tendency to lung cancer also have a hereditary tendency to smoke cigarettes. It is true that smoking habits of identical twins are more alike than those of non-identical twins, so that there may be an hereditary basis for the desire to smoke, and that there is a variety of differences in personality and traits and habits between smokers and non-smokers (see paragraph 79). This hypothesis would imply, of course, that the hereditary tendencies both to smoke and to develop lung cancer are quantitatively related and that the tendency to give up smoking as well as the tendency to smoke is hereditarily determined. To explain the increase in lung cancer in recent years Fisher does not propose that there has been a sudden simultaneous development of inherited liability to lung cancer in many different countries, but that smokers have an inherited susceptibility to some other unidentified environmental influence which has recently arisen in every country in which the incidence of lung cancer has increased. This indefinite hypothesis is unsatisfactory in itself and is also difficult to reconcile with a recent comparison between Seventh Day Adventists and a control group in California[206]. The members of this sect are all non-smokers. The observed incidence of cancer of the lung among them was one-eighth of the control incidence. Moreover, in contrast to the controls, in whom the incidence of lung cancer was much higher in men than in women, the incidence in the Adventists was equal in the two sexes. Cancer of other sites (except the mouth, larynx and oesophagus which are also associated with smoking) occurred with equal frequency in Adventists and controls so that the Adventists had no general immunity from cancer. The only two male Adventists with lung cancer were both converts who had been cigarette smokers until middle age. It is inconceivable that those born into one religious sect, but not those converted to it, should inherit a low susceptibility to lung cancer.

(v) In support of the hereditary or constitutional hypothesis Berkson[13, 14] has stressed the large number of diseases by which smokers have been shown to be excessively affected and has suggested that non-smokers are a highly selected group who are "biologically self-protective", and endowed with "robustness in meeting mortal stress from disease generally", while Eysenck *et al*[70] stress the "accelerated rate of living" of cigarette smokers as a possible explanation of their higher death rates. This hypothesis fails to account for the disproportionate increase in death rates among smokers from lung cancer compared with other causes.* Berkson's objections based on his disinclination to believe that smoking could by itself increase death rates from several different diseases have been well answered in a cogent review[41] from the U.S. Department of Health, Education and Welfare which points out that there is "nothing contradictory nor inconsistent in the suggestion that one agent can be responsible for more than one disease . . . The great fog of London in 1952 increased the death rate for a number of causes, particularly respiratory and coronary disease, but no one has given this as a reason for doubting the causal role of the Fog . . . A universe in which cause and effect always have a one-to-one correspondence with each other would be easier to understand but it obviously is not the kind we inhabit."

(vi) Since there is generally held to be a correlation between heavy smoking and heavy drinking, it has been suggested that alcohol might be the common factor associated with both smoking and lung cancer. But it has been shown that the association of lung cancer with smoking is independent of alcohol consumption[51, 94, 202].

(vii) The possibility that motor vehicle exhausts might be an important cause of the recent increase in incidence of lung cancer can be rejected since there is no increase in lung cancer death rates among road haulage workers, who would be expected to have excessive exposure to such exhaust gases[19, 50].

(viii) The question of the role of general air pollution is more complex. The relationship of smoking with lung cancer has been shown to hold in both rural and urban areas, but death-rates from lung cancer are higher in urban than in rural areas[45, 185]. These differences can be accounted for only in part by differences in smoking habits between inhabitants of urban and rural areas[51, 184]. Interpreta-

* Berkson insists that the proper measure of an effect of smoking is not the ratio of death rates of smokers to those of non-smokers but the absolute number of excess deaths. Most people believe that the ratio is more relevant to questions of causation.

tion of epidemiological data in relation to the relative importance of smoking and air pollution is as yet uncertain. On the one hand there is the observation that the death rate from lung cancer in Finland has been the second highest in Europe and only slightly less than in Britain, although the population is largely rural and there appears to have been little air pollution. The people have long been heavy cigarette smokers and this suggests that smoking is more important than air pollution. On the other hand there are observations in South Africa[49] and in New Zealand[64] which show that at the same level of smoking, immigrants from the United Kingdom have higher rates of lung cancer than native-born men, suggesting that some persistent effect of exposure to an environmental factor during early life in the United Kingdom may many years later have led to a higher incidence of lung cancer among the immigrants. Similarly, from the United States there is evidence that immigrants from Norway have a lower and from the United Kingdom a higher lung cancer death-rate for the same level of smoking than native-born Americans[88]: the rates for the immigrants are intermediate between those for their countries of origin and destination. This observation suggests that exposure to some environmental factor in early life, greater in the United Kingdom and less in Scandinavia than in the United States, increases the incidence of lung cancer, and if this is accepted, the presumption that this factor is general air pollution is strong. In Britain the social classes differ in their lung cancer death rates in a manner similar to their differences in cigarette consumption, except that there is a relative deficiency of deaths in social classes I and II. Whereas social classes I and II have a death rate from lung cancer lower than that of classes III and V, their cigarette consumption is about the same.* This might be due to differences in exposure to air pollution[183], since it has been found that the social class composition of county boroughs is strongly correlated with air pollution from domestic and industrial sources[149]. Although general air pollution appears to increase the incidence of lung cancer, it is hard to see how its effects could account for the great increase in lung cancer death rates in the last three decades, or for the greater number of deaths in men than in women; while both these effects may be accounted for by changes in cigarette smoking. The interaction of air pollution and smoking requires further investigation, but it is clear that at all levels of air pollution cigarette smokers suffer a risk of lung cancer which increases with the number

* The Figures for 1949-53 are as follows:

Social Class	I	II	III	IV	V
Index of daily cigarette consumption[189]	100	101	108	92	104
Lung cancer mortality (percent of all men)[168]	81	82	107	91	118

24

of cigarettes smoked, and even in the most rural areas in this country heavy cigarette smokers develop lung cancer 15 to 20 times as frequently as non-smokers[51, 184].

33. We are therefore left with the hypothesis that habitual cigarette smoking over many years is a cause, in the ordinary sense, of lung cancer. It is important to recognise that the hypothesis is not that cigarette smoking is the *only* cause of lung cancer. The fact that the disease does, rarely, occur in non-smokers, and the effects of air pollution and various industrial hazards[52, 105] clearly indicate that other factors are concerned. Nor does the fact that only a minority of smokers develop lung cancer negate the hypothesis any more than does the fact that only a minority of persons exposed to tuberculous infection develop tuberculosis negate the hypothesis that exposure to infection is a cause of the disease. The minority response only indicates that other factors determine susceptibility. There are however several gaps and apparent discrepancies in the evidence which require further consideration.

34. Although there is a high correlation between cigarette consumption and standardised death-rates from lung cancer in countries for which the figures are available, the death-rates for Japan and the U.S.A. are lower than would be expected[53]. One explanation of the relatively low death-rate in the U.S.A. has already been suggested, namely the tendency of Americans to throw away the stubs of cigarettes when they are still quite long; the low rate in Japan remains unexplained. White male South Africans also have a much lower lung cancer death-rate than would be expected from their cigarette consumption[49].

35. Fisher[75] has pointed out that in Doll and Hill's retrospective study there appeared to be a paradoxical effect of inhaling, because a smaller proportion of the heavier smokers among the lung cancer patients than of those among the control patients said that they inhaled. The effect of inhaling on the site of deposition of the particulate matter of tobacco smoke in the bronchial tree is complex however, and may be affected by the way in which the smoke is inhaled[46]. In three other surveys[19, 132, 174] a higher proportion of inhalers has been found among cigarette smokers with lung cancer than among control smokers without lung cancer. It seems that more evidence about the effect of inhaling is required especially since in their recent extensive study of this question Schwartz and colleagues[176] found that inhaling appeared to increase the liability of light smokers to lung cancer while this effect was less evident in heavy smokers. The probability is that most heavy cigarette smokers inhale.

36. Table II, p. 14 shows that the mortality from lung cancer has increased in men more than in women, whereas it can be seen in Figure 1,

p. 3 that increases in tobacco consumption have been proportionately greater in women. It is probably too early to judge the effect of the recent steep increase in cigarette consumption by women. Until 1940 their consumption of cigarettes was less than a tenth of the male consumption and it only increased sharply during World War II. Since the hypothesis under consideration is that smoking causes lung cancer after many years, this increase in female cigarette smoking would not yet be expected to show its full effect. The difference between male and female death rates from lung cancer has decreased in the younger age groups[101] as would be expected if the relatively recent adoption of cigarette smoking by women were beginning to take effect.

37. Skin cancer can be produced in mice by applications of tar condensed from tobacco smoke[69, 204, 207] but the results obtained by various investigators have not been uniform[199] and exposure of animals to tobacco smoke in inhaled air has failed to produce lung cancers[87, 90, 158]. Moreover the amount of cancer-producing substances in the smoke itself does not seem likely to be sufficient to account for the large number of cases of cancer associated with the habit[37, 208].

38. These facts are sometimes used to support the statement that there is no proof that lung cancer is caused by cigarette smoke; but this would imply that the cause of human disease can only be demonstrated by animal experiment. If tobacco smoke had been shown to cause cancer in animals the causative hypothesis would have been strengthened, but it can still stand without this support.

39. In addition to the known carcinogens which have been detected in tobacco smoke[40, 63, 114, 137] others as yet undetected may be present; possibly two or more in combination may reinforce each other in producing cancer. It is possible that tobacco smoke may contain substances which act in conjunction with substances generally present in the air we breathe to produce cancer, although neither substances might do so alone[82, 83]. Indeed the action of tobacco might be simply to produce chronic irritation which, as in other tissues, may increase liability of the lung to cancer[159]. There is a wide field for further investigation here, but no ground for refuting the evidence from human experience.

40. It is perhaps relevant here to recall that the great sanitary movement in the mid-nineteenth century began to bring infective diseases such as cholera and typhoid under control long before the germs that caused these diseases were discovered. The movement was based on observations such as that drinking polluted water was associated with disease. If the provision of clean water had had to await the discovery of bacteria, preventable deaths, numbered in thousands, would have continued to occur for many years.

Conclusion

41. The strong statistical association between smoking, especially of cigarettes, and lung cancer is most simply explained on a causal basis. This is supported by compatible, though not conclusive, laboratory and pathological evidence namely (a) the presence of several substances known to be capable of producing cancer in tobacco smoke; (b) the production of cancer of the skin in animals by repeated application of tobacco tar; and (c) the finding, in the bronchial epithelium of smokers, of microscopic changes of the kind which may precede the development of cancer. The conclusion that smoking is an important cause of lung cancer implies that if the habit ceased, the death rate from lung cancer would eventually fall to a fraction, perhaps to one fifth[65] or even, among men, to one tenth[53] of the present level. Since the present annual number of deaths attributed to lung cancer before the age of retirement is some 12,000 (Table V, p. 47) a large amount of premature shortening of life is at issue.

SMOKING AND OTHER LUNG DISEASES

Smoking and Chronic Bronchitis

42. Bronchitis, especially in its chronic form, is one of the major causes of disablement and death in Britain particularly among middle aged and elderly men. In 1959 among men aged 45 to 64, 5,966 deaths (8·0% of all male deaths) were attributed to bronchitis and its complications, and in women of the same age there were 1,316 deaths (2·9% of all female deaths) from this cause. Some 27 million working days are lost to industry each year because of bronchitis. It is of great public health importance to consider how much of this toll may be attributed to smoking.

43. To this end the way in which the disease develops may be recalled[76]. At first there is simply persistent or recurrent cough with production of phlegm. Infection of the bronchial tubes is manifest by recurrent illnesses in which the phlegm becomes discoloured or purulent and in time persistent breathlessness may develop. Both the infection and the breathlessness, which is often due to an associated emphysema*, tend to increase in severity and persistence. In many cases heart failure develops and death usually occurs during an exacerbation of infection.

44. **Smoking and productive cough**. It is common experience—the popular term is "smoker's cough"—that smoking causes cough and expectoration, and the validity of this simple observation has been

---

* A condition in which the air spaces in the lung enlarge and break down so that respiration is interfered with.

27

confirmed by many investigations both in samples of the general population and in hospital patients[78, 99, 161]. These have shown that cough and expectoration become more prevalent the more cigarettes are smoked (Figure 11). It is also common experience that most people with a smoker's cough lose this symptom when they stop smoking, and population surveys all agree that ex-smokers expectorate less than smokers. Pipe and cigar smokers are found to be affected much less often than cigarette smokers[154, 161].

45. Thus in many people, cigarette smoke appears to act as a bronchial irritant causing cough and increased secretion of bronchial mucus which is coughed up as phlegm, but the irritation is often reversible. In experimental animals, acute exposure of the bronchial tubes to cigarette smoke causes an out-pouring of mucus with slowing of ciliary movement*[7, 44, 100]. These are changes which, in man, would be expected to result in productive cough. Pathological evidence of chronic bronchitis is found more frequently in smokers than in non-smokers at autopsy, and more frequently in heavier than in lighter smokers[5, 6, 30, 106, 173].

46. **Smoking and disabling bronchitis.** Population surveys have shown that recurrent chest illnesses (Figure 11), and breathlessness[99], are found more in cigarette smokers than in non-smokers or pipe smokers, but heavier smokers have not always been found to be more frequently affected than lighter smokers or ex-smokers. The complete syndrome of chronic bronchitis, however, has been found to be closely related quantitatively to smoking habits[35, 66] and some studies have indicated that men and women with similar smoking habits are equally affected by the disease, so that the higher incidence in men may be largely due to their heavier smoking[77, 155]. Patients admitted to hospital with chronic bronchitis have been found to be much heavier smokers than control patients of the same age and sex and it has been estimated that heavy smokers are five times more likely to be admitted to hospital with bronchitis than non-smokers[65, 131]. The chest infections which may follow major abdominal operations occur with much greater frequency in smokers than in non-smokers[150].

47. **Smoking and function of the lungs.** Smoking does not have any marked immediate effect on lung function in most people[4]. But by sensitive methods an increased resistance to air flow in the bronchial tubes may be detected after inhaling cigarette smoke[151]. Many studies have shown that the lungs of smokers are on the average impaired compared with non-smokers, particularly in respect of resistance to bronchial air flow[17, 67, 79, 213]. This impairment has even been observed in smokers who have no symptoms of bronchitis[194]. In popula-

* See footnote to paragraph 20.

28

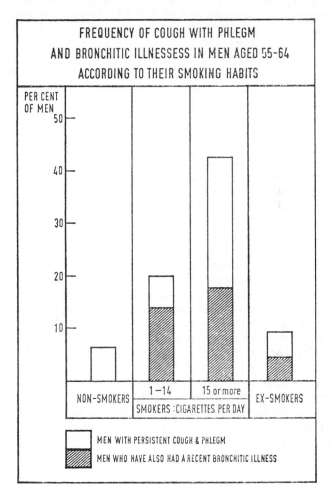

FIGURE 11   THE FREQUENCY OF COUGH WITH PHLEGM AND BRONCHITIC ILLNESS
IN MEN AGED 55-64 STUDIED IN THREE SURVEYS IN GREAT BRITAIN.

These figures, taken from surveys of men in Wales, Lancashire and Scotland by
Higgins[99], show that cough and phlegm are much more frequent in smokers,
especially in heavier smokers, than in non-smokers or ex-smokers. The hatched part
of the columns represents the percentage of men who had had a bronchitic illness
causing loss of time from work of a week or more in the previous three years. These
illnesses were also more frequent in the smokers but there was less difference between
lighter and heavier smokers. Some of the ex-smokers may have given up smoking
because of their symptoms but still have had bronchitis.

29

tion studies greater impairment has been found in cigarette smokers than in pipe or cigar smokers, but, as with the symptom of breathlessness, heavier smokers have not usually been found to be more affected than lighter smokers[78, 99, 154].

48. **Mortality studies.** Among British doctors, Doll and Hill[57] found a steady increase of bronchitis death rates with increasingly heavy smoking, those smoking more than 25 cigarettes a day having a death rate from bronchitis six times greater than that of non-smokers. In the U.S.A. Dorn[62] found that deaths from bronchitis and emphysema were more than three times as frequent in regular cigarette smokers as in non-smokers.

49. **Other factors besides smoking.** The strong association between smoking, especially cigarette smoking, and the incidence of chronic bronchitis does not necessarily mean that cigarette smoking is the chief cause or only cause of the disease. There is ample evidence implicating other factors:—

(i) Bronchitis seems to have been an important cause of death in this country before the advent of the relatively modern habit of cigarette smoking, and there has been no dramatic increase in death rates from this disease since cigarette smoking has become widespread (Figure 7, p. 15). There has, however, been no reduction in deaths from bronchitis with the advent of antibiotics as there has been in deaths from pneumonia and tuberculosis, so that a reduction in deaths from bronchitis due to antibiotics may be masking an increase due to cigarette smoking.

(ii) The death rate from bronchitis is five times as great in unskilled labourers (social class V) as in professional men (social class I), although there is very little social class gradient in tobacco consumption (see footnote p. 24).

(iii) An important effect of atmospheric pollution is indicated by a higher prevalence of bronchitis in towns than in country districts, and by significant associations which have been found between death and sickness-absence rates from bronchitis and various indices of air pollution[45, 71, 185].

(iv) Death rates from bronchitis in middle aged men in the United Kingdom are many times greater than in the U.S.A.[76] Since cigarette consumption is similar in the two countries, factors other than smoking must be implicated. Part of the explanation may be the differences in diagnostic terms used in the two countries, but the experience of physicians who have worked in both countries leaves no doubt that chronic bronchitis is much more prevalent in the United Kingdom than in the U.S.A.

50. In summary, smoking, and especially cigarette smoking, often causes productive cough. This is as true in the U.S.A. as in the

United Kingdom. It is reasonable to assume that this productive cough predisposes to the disabling and fatal forms of chronic bronchitis under the influence of other aetiological factors, which are more prevalent in towns and in the lower social classes. Cigarette smoking should thus be regarded as an important conditioning factor rendering many men and women liable to a disabling disease which they might have escaped had they not smoked.

Smoking and Pulmonary Tuberculosis

51. The incidence of pulmonary tuberculosis in Britain declined gradually during the first half of the 20th century (with minor increases associated with the two world wars), while cigarette smoking increased. Since the introduction of streptomycin and other drugs that are effective against tuberculosis, the rate of decline of death rates has been rapid, and rather fewer new cases have been notified; but this favourable trend has been much less marked in elderly men. The continued high toll in this age and sex group, in which heavy smoking is most likely to show its effect, is the most striking feature of recent tuberculosis statistics.

52. In 1956 Lowe[138] found a significant association of smoking with tuberculosis in men and women over the age of 30 when he compared the smoking habits of tuberculosis patients with control subjects of the same age and sex without tuberculosis in Birmingham. From these figures it has been estimated[65] that the risk of requiring treatment for tuberculosis is four times as great in heavy smokers as in non-smokers. Recent evidence, however, has suggested that there may be a closer association with alcohol consumption than with cigarette smoking in cases of tuberculosis[212] so that the association with smoking may not be causal. More evidence of the association of tuberculosis with smoking is needed before its significance can be assessed.

SMOKING AND DISEASES OF THE HEART AND BLOOD VESSELS

Smoking and Coronary Heart Disease

53. There is little doubt that in some patients with coronary* heart disease, anginal pain† may be brought on by smoking[162], presumably owing to the increased amount of blood that the heart puts out and the consequent increase in the work it has to do (for measurements of

---

* The coronary arteries are those which carry blood to the muscles of the heart itself.

† Anginal pain is that produced when the heart is deprived of a blood supply adequate for the work it has to do.

the cardiac output show that this may increase on smoking[214]). Changes in the pattern of electrical changes in the heart suggestive of reduced coronary blood flow may follow smoking even in the absence of anginal pain[125, 142, 170, 171] and there is some evidence that smoking may increase liability to disturbances of the cardiac rhythm[23].

54. In recent years many investigations have been concerned with the possibility that, apart from aggravating the symptoms of coronary heart disease, smoking, particularly cigarette smoking, may play a part in its causation and may thus be one of the reasons for the increase of this disease which has taken place in western countries since World War I. In several investigations[21, 57, 62, 94, 210] an association between smoking habits and deaths from coronary disease has been shown. Table III, p. 34, from Doll and Hill's investigation of British doctors, shows a considerable increase in coronary death rates with increasing tobacco consumption in men under 55 years of age but there is no consistent difference between non-smokers, light and heavier smokers in the older men. These findings are similar to those of other recent studies, that the main association between smoking and coronary disease occurs during early middle age. Figure 12 from Hammond and Horn's study in the U.S.A. also shows that there is a substantial reduction in mortality from coronary heart disease in those who give up smoking. The U.S. figures show no increased risk in cigar and pipe smokers compared with non-smokers. The British figures show a similar trend but there were too few men who only smoked pipes or cigars for the difference to be established.

55. Recent figures from the long term prospective study of coronary disease in the New England town of Framingham[48] suggests an association between heavy smoking and the onset of the disease in its more serious forms as well as with mortality. In this study the effect of smoking seemed to have no association with high blood pressure and increase in blood fats which also increase the risk of the disease. In several studies, however, smokers have been shown to have slightly raised levels of cholesterol and other blood fats which may be associated with an increased liability to coronary disease[84, 113].

56. Although coronary heart disease is the main contributor to the excess mortality of cigarette smokers observed in all the prospective studies, it is not possible to assert, as in the case of lung cancer, that the association between coronary disease and smoking is causal. Lung cancer is rare in non-smokers[197], the disease is associated with cigarette smoking at all ages and no personal characteristic other than smoking has been shown to increase liability to it. In contrast, coronary heart disease frequently affects non-

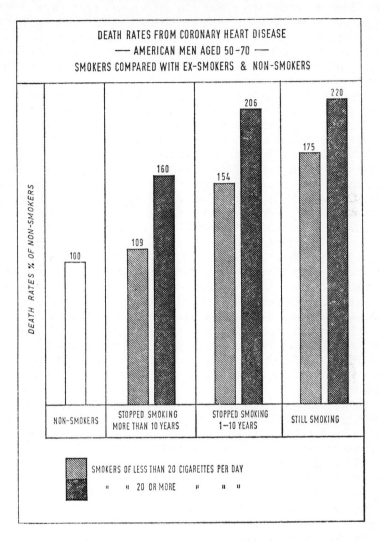

FIGURE 12 THE RELATIONSHIP OF DEATH RATES FROM CORONARY HEART DISEASE
TO SMOKING HABITS.

These figures are taken from the American prospective study by Hammond and
Horn.[94] The death rate of heavy smokers was twice that of non-smokers and even
after they had given up for more than ten years the rate was still half as much again as
for non-smokers. In the lighter smokers the excess was still considerable but those
who had given up for more than ten years had a death rate nearly the same as that
of non-smokers.

TABLE III

DEATH RATES PER 100,000 FROM CORONARY HEART DISEASE AMONG BRITISH DOCTORS IN RELATION TO SMOKING HABITS.*
(NUMBERS OF DEATHS IN EACH GROUP IN BRACKETS)

Age	Non-smokers	Smokers of cigarettes only			Other smokers (past and present)		
		1-14/day	15-24/day	25 or more/day	1-14 grams/day	15-24 grams/day	25 grams or more/day
35-54	44 (8)	100 (13)	161 (25)	202 (24)	88 (9)	110 (7)	119 (4)
55-64	734 (14)	850 (27)	541 (22)	820 (27)	507 (16)	246 (7)	483 (9)
65-74	1,113 (12)	1,303 (29)	1,054 (20)	1,506 (20)	908 (27)	1,052 (21)	1,456 (14)
75+	1,518 (13)	2,116 (32)	1,230 (11)	1,744 (6)	1,928 (47)	3,047 (32)	3,179 (12)

* From Doll and Hill[57, 58]

smokers. The association with smoking is only clear in middle age, and various other factors such as mental strain, sedentary occupation and indulgence in fatty foods[160], which are thought to increase liability to coronary thrombosis, are also commonly associated with heavy smoking. It is possible that factors such as these may be responsible as much as smoking itself for increased mortality from this disease among smokers. A recent French retrospective study[175] of the relationship between smoking and coronary heart disease has, however, shown a significant relationship between this disease and a history of inhaling during smoking. Inhalation was less frequent in the older than in the younger subjects, so that this factor may account for the closer association of smoking with coronary disease in younger than in older subjects. This association with inhaling increases the likelihood that cigarette smoking and coronary disease may be causally related.

57. Although much more investigation is needed to assess these complex interacting factors it seems sensible at present to agree with the recent statement of the Committee on Smoking and Cardiovascular Disease of the American Heart Association[2] that the present evidence "strongly suggests that heavy cigarette smoking may contribute to or accelerate the development of coronary disease or its complications", at least in men under the age of fifty-five.

Smoking and Other Diseases of the Heart and Blood Vessels

58. There appears to be wide agreement that smoking is an important cause of thromboangiitis obliterans*. This disease hardly ever occurs in non-smokers and its progression is unfavourably affected by continuance of smoking[127]. There is some inconclusive evidence that sensitivity to tobacco may be concerned in the development of this disease[178]. Apart from coronary disease, the American studies have shown moderate increases in death rates from other conditions that are associated with arterial disease[62, 93, 94].

59. Although the immediate effect of nicotine on the blood pressure is to raise it there is no evidence of any long term effect of this kind. Indeed epidemiological studies have shown that the mean blood pressure of cigarette smokers tends to be slightly but significantly lower than that of non-smokers. Pipe smokers have been found to have intermediate levels[66, 113]. Ex-smokers in one survey had the same average pressure as those who had never smoked[48].

---

* A disease in which blood-flow is impaired, chiefly in the vessels of the legs.

SMOKING AND GASTRO-INTESTINAL DISEASES

60. That the consumption of tobacco has undeniable reactions on the stomach and intestines is within the experience of most smokers. Apart from the nausea and vomiting that may follow the first smoke of a life-time and which are probably due to central nervous stimulation, perhaps the best known effect on the digestive system of established smokers is alleviation of hunger. Inhibition of gastric hunger contractions has been observed after a few puffs of a cigarette. The increase in weight which commonly occurs after forsaking the habit of smoking[20] and the fact that non-smokers are on the average 3-4% heavier and fatter than smokers[113] may be partly due to this alleviation of hunger. In American medical students, however, a higher proportion of heavier individuals were found in smokers than in non-smokers[187]. This may be a characteristic of younger smokers. Most physicians have seen an adverse affect of heavy smoking on patients with gastric or duodenal ulcers and those with colon spasm. By increasing the activity of the colon, smoking may stimulate movement of the bowels.

61. Various investigators have studied the influence of smoking on the movements and secretions of the stomach and intestine. With gastric activity in general the findings have been variable but a trend towards a reduction of activity has usually been found. The response varies from person to person. Using intra-gastric balloons to record activity Batterman[10] found three types of response in normal people after smoking one cigarette. One third showed complete cessation of activity for a period varying from a few minutes to a few hours. Another third was unaffected, and in the remainder the activity of the stomach was first stimulated and then depressed. Exactly the same pattern of response has been found after the smoking of one cigarette in patients with peptic ulceration. It was also noted that two cigarettes might cause increased activity and bring on pain, whereas one had no effect. Other observers have found no significant effect of smoking on the movements of the stomach[38]. Similar variation is found in secretion of acid by the stomach. Some patients with peptic ulcer have a relatively small increase in secretion of acid after smoking.

62. The significance of smoking in functional disorders of digestion has been studied among 300 smokers complaining of heartburn, eructation, loss of appetite, nausea, flatulence and abdominal discomfort; these symptoms were greatly alleviated in the majority by stopping smoking[85]. One American study[11] of the effect of smoking on the medical management of ulcers in 108 patients showed that those who continued to smoke had a poor response to anti-acid

therapy and this was associated with a high incidence of acute exacerbations. On the other hand, those who stopped or who were non-smokers, responded well and had a lower incidence of acute exacerbations.

63. The effect of smoking on the rate of healing of gastric ulcers has been carefully recorded, in a controlled study in Britain[61]. Hospital patients with gastric ulcer were divided into two groups, all being smokers. The first group were advised to stop and the second were not. Otherwise they had the same four weeks' medical treatment in bed. Among the 40 patients who were advised to stop smoking, most of whom did so, there was an average reduction in the size of the ulcer by 78% and this compared with 57% for those who continued to smoke. The differences were significant and it was concluded that smoking interferes with healing and promotes chronicity of ulceration. It was notable that in a proportion of patients who continued to smoke, the ulcer actually increased in size while this deterioration was not observed in any of those who gave up smoking.

64. In the prospective mortality studies of Doll and Hill[57], Dorn[62], Hammond and Horn[94], an increased mortality from peptic ulcer was found in smokers of all kinds (cigarettes, pipe and cigars), the smokers having nearly three times the mortality of non-smokers. Hammond and Horn found no evidence that this was due to associated respiratory disease. In a study of men over 60 years old in Birmingham[66], the prevalence of peptic ulcer was about 50% higher in cigarette smokers than in non-smokers and pipe smokers.

65. Smoking does not appear to be a cause of ulcers in the stomach and duodenum but probably exacerbates and perpetuates them. The disease certainly occurs in non-smokers and during the past three decades, during which tobacco consumption in the United Kingdom has increased, the incidence of gastric ulcer has diminished. The prevalence of duodenal ulcer has considerably increased, but the world distribution of mortality from duodenal ulcer is quite unlike the world distribution of tobacco smoking.

66. Various investigators have found an association between smoking (of cigarettes, pipes and cigars) and cancer of the mouth, larynx and oesophagus. These forms of cancer are also associated with a high alcohol intake, which is also correlated with smoking so that it is difficult to interpret the evidence[62, 94, 174, 201, 202, 203].

SMOKING AND OTHER CONDITIONS

Cancer of the Urinary Tract

67. Both in restrospective and prospective studies a significant association between smoking and cancer of the bladder (only in men)

and in some, but not all studies, an association with cancer of the prostate has been found[62, 94, 136, 176]. Significantly more inhalers have been found among cigarette smokers with cancer of the bladder than in the control subjects[176].

Cirrhosis of the Liver
68. Heavy drinking is an important cause of this disease, so that the increased mortality from cirrhosis of the liver in smokers which was shown in both American prospective studies[62, 94] is probably due to the fact that most heavy drinkers are also smokers.

Diseases of the Central Nervous System
69. Tobacco amblyopia (a rare form of blindness affecting heavy smokers) has been noted in association with malnutrition. Recent evidence has shown a clear association with Vitamin B_{12} deficiency, which appears to render the optic nerve more vulnerable to tobacco[96]. Several other neurological disturbances have been attributed to tobacco but most reports are of isolated cases or are poorly documented[126].

Industrial Accidents and Injuries
70. Explosions in coal mines causing injury and loss of life have been attributed to illicit cigarette smoking underground. In a factory in Birmingham, Lowe[140] found that attendance of the younger workers for the treatment of injuries was more frequent in smokers than in non-smokers. There was little difference between smokers and non-smokers over the age of 35 in this respect. He suggested that this might be due to smokers being temperamentally more accident prone than non-smokers, a possibility supported by a variety of studies that have shown psychological differences between smokers and non-smokers (see paragraph 79). The possibility of accidents being a direct consequence of smoking was not excluded.

Parental Smoking and Children's Birth Weight
71. In four investigations[79a, 139, 179, 209] the birth weight of children whose mothers smoked during pregnancy was less than that of children born to non-smoking mothers. The reason for this is obscure—in one study, indeed, the proportion of underweight babies bore a closer relationship to the father's than to the mother's smoking habits when both were smokers[209]. There does not appear to be any clinical significance in these differences. There is no difference in the frequency of complications of pregnancy and labour between smokers and non-smokers, nor of malformation of the babies. Indeed, because of the smaller size of babies born to smoking mothers the need for surgical induction of labour is less. These observations may be relevant

to the fact that the incidence of premature birth as defined by birth weight has not declined during recent years. While obstetrical services have been steadily improving, the proportion of women who smoke has been increasing.

Smoking and Athletic Performance

72. Athletes customarily abstain from smoking because of a widespread belief that it is "bad for the wind", but examples are known of eminent athletes who have continued to smoke during training without any apparent adverse effect on their performance. Very little research appears to have been carried out on this subject, probably because of the difficulties both of assessing performance and of persuading subjects to change their smoking habits at the request of investigators. In one study of thirteen subjects[112] the time taken to complete a stint of vigorous bicycling was significantly less during non-smoking periods in five out of thirteen students. This suggests that in some but not all subjects smoking impairs athletic performance. The impaired function of the lungs in smokers compared with non-smokers (paragraph 47) would also suggest that smoking is likely on the average to impair capacity for strenuous exertion.

THE PSYCHOLOGICAL ASPECT OF SMOKING

73. On the psychological aspect of smoking there is extremely little exact information. Widespread popular beliefs (which doctors mostly share) credit smoking with the ability to relieve tension and assume that it is, or at any rate can become, an addictive habit. It is certainly a difficult habit to break and disagreeable withdrawal symptoms are often experienced. Since smoking is so widespread, it is supposed that it partially satisfies some common human need, as alcohol is thought to do: but evidence pointing to any such specific need, or demonstrating unsatisfied need in those who have never smoked or who cease to smoke has not been found.

74. The pattern of smoking in the two sexes at different ages described in paragraphs 7 and 8, and other minor differences between various social and occupational groups throw little or no light on motivation. The commonest reasons given by children for starting smoking are that they wanted to satisfy their curiosity, that they wished to be like others, or simply that they were given a cigarette[18]. Studies in both American and British schoolchildren[28, 104] and young adults[115, 144] have shown significant associations between their frequency of smoking and the smoking habits of parents or siblings. The children of parents who smoke are twice as likely to smoke as children of non-smoking or ex-smoking parents, children with one

smoking parent being intermediate. In England, secondary modern schoolchildren smoke more than grammar schoolchildren[186]. More intelligent children smoke less than their duller fellows. Fewer children smoke who are aware of the health hazards than those who are unaware of these hazards[28].

75. Cultural factors undoubtedly play a large part in smoking as they do in coffee drinking, taking tea or alcohol, and other such habits. Different ways of enjoying tobacco (snuff, chewing, pipe, cigars, cigarettes, nargileh) in different countries, its incorporation in social usages and rituals, its varying accessibility to minors and women, the social approval or penalties it entails, the changing pattern in different periods—all bespeak its dependence on the prevailing culture.

76. Smokers claim that smoking produces a sense of relaxation in their leisure hours and helps them to concentrate when they are working[143]. It is virtually impossible to test this claim by experiment. Smokers differ from non-smokers both intellectually and in other psychological respects so that differences in the average intellectual performance of the two groups cannot be validly attributed to the effects of smoking. Tests of confirmed smokers after deprivation or of non-smokers after heavy smoking are inevitably confused by the wide variety of pharmacological effects induced by such abrupt changes. In some studies nicotine has been credited[33, 97] with a favourable effect on visual imagery and a shortening of reaction time for arithmetical or other psychological tasks: in others an unfavourable result has been reported. It is likely that the contribution of the smoker's personality to his subjective response to smoking may be as important as any direct pharmacological effects on his nervous system.

77. There is abundant evidence that some anxious people smoke very heavily but so do some people who manifest no anxiety. In a study of 252 Harvard graduates[141]. it seemed that heavy smokers tended to smoke more when under pressure, but that only a minority of light smokers behaved in this way. Heavy smokers in another American group[130] reported more neurotic symptoms and traits indicative of anxiety than did moderate smokers. In an Italian study[177], smoking a cigarette brought about changes in the pattern of electrical activity of skeletal muscle, but not of a kind to indicate relaxation. At present, in default of sufficient data, it can be assumed that smoking is one of the many permissible forms of alternative outlet for people who are frightened, keyed-up, expectant or bored[144].

78. Various opinions[1, 80] have been put forward regarding dynamic or unconscious forces which may cause smoking to be so widely adopted and enjoyed. The early psychoanalysts[72, 181] regarded it as a substitute gratification closely connected with oral needs and they

stressed its connection with masculinity, deprivation of the maternal breast at weaning, and the taboo-like restriction of the habit to adults. Other psychoanalysts have stressed the compulsive aspects of the smoker's behaviour and his unconscious pleasure in setting things alight[102, 157].

79. The intrinsic or constitutional factors which lead people to smoke, and to smoke very heavily, were studied by comparing small numbers of heavy smokers and non-smokers in one American study[95]. The heavy smokers were of a restless, ardent, energetic personality, the non-smokers steadier, more dependable, quieter. In another recent American study[135] cigarette smokers were found to have changed jobs more often, moved more often, entered hospital more often, and participated in sports more often than non-smokers; on a psychological test, their responses were more neurotic than those of non-smokers. In a British survey[70] of 2,360 men selected according to their age, social class and smoking habits, cigarette smokers were found to be more extraverted than non-smokers, while pipe smokers were the most introverted group. It was suggested that these findings indicated genotypic differences between non-smokers, cigarette smokers and pipe smokers. That differences in smoking habits may be in part due to a hereditary disposition is supported by four studies[74, 81, 166, 190] which have shown that identical twins are more significantly concordant in smoking habits than non-identical twins —a contrast which is not due to greater similarity of environment of the former for it is discernible when the identical twins have been brought up apart.

80. It has been reported that injections of nicotine can relieve the desire for a cigarette when smoking is abruptly stopped[109] and the oral administration of lobeline has been shown to provide some substitutive relief and may assist smokers to give up the habit[9, 167]. The discomforts that ensue when smoking is stopped may thus be genuine withdrawal symptoms due to addiction to nicotine[108], but are also those to be expected when any well-established and pleasant habit is discontinued, particularly one which has become a valued element in everyday life and is regarded as a prop or solace.

81. Very little is known about the psychological factors that lead people to discontinue smoking. Considerations of finance and health are most often given as reasons, but such considerations are often much in the mind of smokers who nevertheless do not give up the habit[26]. That more than remote awareness of the hazards of smoking is needed to induce a change of habit is suggested by the contrast between the smoking habits of doctors and the general public (Figure 4, p. 9). There can be little doubt that most of the doctors who have given up smoking in recent years (Figure 5, p. 11) have done so be-

41

cause they have accepted the evidence that the habit can cause serious disease. There is no evidence in this country as to whether those doctors who specialise in chest and heart diseases smoke less than their colleagues, but a suggestion of an effect of close acquaintance with the consequences of smoking was given by an American study[129] in which the smoking habits of 72 scientists concerned with lung cancer were compared with those of 72 experimental psychologists. 33% of the lung cancer experts who had smoked in the past five years had stopped, compared with only 18% of the psychologists, and at the time of the enquiry 70% of the former were non-smokers and only 7% were heavy smokers (more than 20 cigarettes a day), while the figures for the psychologists were 47% non-smokers and 28% heavy smokers.

82. In another American study[89], it was found that the proportion of smokers who gave up the habit varied in different social and economic groups; the rate was highest for professional workers and farmers, lowest for unskilled manual labourers. In the same study an inverse relationship was found between the discontinuance rate and the proportion of regular smokers in the population as a whole, which suggests that "when social forces tend to militate against adoption of the smoking habit by members of the group, these same forces persist to motivate discontinuance by some, after the habit has been formed". This conclusion, if warranted, is important since it emphasises social factors, such as approval, rather than internal drives and needs that are usually assumed to lead people to smoke. No doubt both operate and can either reinforce or nullify each other. The parallel with alcoholism is close. While many if not the majority of people enjoy alcoholic drinks on relatively infrequent occasions, however, there are very few occasional smokers. Most smokers consume a regular daily amount of tobacco. It appears that smoking is generally much more habit-forming than drinking.

CONCLUSIONS

The Benefits of Smoking

83. There is no evidence that smoking promotes physical health. Its benefits appear to be psychological and social and are hard to express in quantitative terms. Many smokers have written eloquently of the assuagement of irritation and anxiety, the cementing of friendship and the promotion of human intercourse by the "azure vapour" of tobacco. The social value of smoking is widely endorsed. The proffering of a cigarette or tobacco pouch constitutes a gesture of friendship between strangers, between negotiators or between

assessors and applicants for jobs. The striking increases in tobacco consumption during the two World Wars (Figure 1, p. 3) bear testimony to the demand for smoking under the stress and boredom of wartime. In the First World War, General Pershing cabled to his Government "Tobacco is as indispensable as the daily ration; we must have thousands of tons of it without delay" and tobacco filled the holds of many ships running the gauntlet of U-boats in both World Wars.

84. Dr. Johnson foresaw an increase of madness if smoking should become obsolete, a forecast for which there was and is no factual foundation.* In a Scottish survey[26] about half of smokers who had discontinued the habit reported a change for the better in their health. The adverse effects were a tendency to gain weight, a feeling of irritation, boredom or inability to relax. Only a third of ex-smokers complained of these symptoms and experience shows that they are often transitory although the gain in weight may sometimes be considerable. There is no evidence to suggest that widespread discontinuance or diminution in the habit of smoking would result in any significant increase in neurotic disorders or physical disease.

85. Whatever the benefits of tobacco smoking to those who enjoy it, the habit is distasteful to an important minority and the testimony of many ex-smokers reveals that abstinence brings less feeling of deprivation than was expected. The pleasures of smoking must now be weighed against its dangers.

Smoking as a Cause of Disease

86. The most reasonable conclusions from all the evidence on the association between smoking and disease are: that cigarette smoking is the most likely cause of the recent world-wide increase in deaths from lung cancer, the death rate from which is at present higher in Britain than in any other country in the world; that it is an important predisposing cause of the development of chronic bronchitis, in the absence of which, morbidity and mortality from this common disease would be substantially reduced; and that it may be partly responsible for the persistent tuberculous morbidity and mortality in elderly men.

87. Cigarette smoking probably increases the risk of dying from coronary heart disease, particularly in early middle age. Smoking of any kind may increase symptoms due to arterial disease of the heart or limbs and possibly promotes its development and progression.

88. It does not appear that smoking causes gastric or duodenal ulceration but there is clear evidence that it has an adverse effect on

* He is also quoted by Boswell as saying 'It is a shocking thing, blowing smoke out of one's mouth into other peoples' mouths, eyes and noses and having the same thing done to us'.

TABLE IV

1. *Death rates from all causes per 1,000 per year*

Age	Non-smokers	Smokers of:—		
		1-14/day	15-24/day	25 or more/day
35-44	1·1	1·56	1·55	4·41
45-54	3·7	5·56	7·18	10·19
55-64	12·0	17·69	20·37	25·57
65-74	31·7	47·10	42·09	59·82

2. *Fractional risk of dying from all causes in decades from age 35 to age 74*

Decade	Non-smokers	Smokers of:—		
		1-14/day	15-24/day	25 or more/day
35-44	1 in 90	1 in 64	1 in 65	1 in 23
45-54	1 in 27	1 in 18	1 in 14	1 in 10
55-64	1 in 8	1 in 6	1 in 5	1 in 4
65-74	1 in 3	1 in 2	1 in 2	1 in 2

3. *Percentage of men aged 35 who may expect to die before the age of 65*

Non-smokers · · ·	15%
Smokers of 1-14/day · ·	22%
Smokers of 15-24/day · ·	25%
Smokers of 25/day · ·	33%

4. *Death rates from lung cancer per 1,000 per year*

Age	Non-smokers	Smokers of:—		
		1-14/day	15-24/day	25 or more/day
35-44	0·0*	0·0*	0·0*	0·12
45-54	0·0*	0·41	0·55	0·58
55-64	0·0*	0·63	1·96	4·29
65-74	0·0*	2·9	4·72	6·04

5. *Fractional risk of dying from lung cancer in decades from age 35 to age 74*

Decade	Non-smokers	Smokers of:—		
		1-14/day	15-24/day	25 or more/day
35-44	—*	—*	—*	1 in 833
45-54	—*	1 in 244	1 in 182	1 in 172
55-64	—*	1 in 159	1 in 51	1 in 23
65-74	—*	1 in 34	1 in 21	1 in 17

healing of these ulcers. This may be one reason for the increased mortality from peptic ulcer among smokers, which has been observed both in the U.S.A. and Britain. Smoking may be a contributory factor in cancer of the mouth, pharynx, oesophagus and bladder.

89. Smoking of pipes and cigars appears to be associated with far less risk than cigarette smoking. It does not seem possible to explain the relative harmlessness of these forms of smoking on any physical or chemical characteristics of the smoke[216]. The contrast with cigarette smoking is probably due to the fact that pipe or cigar smokers seldom inhale[92].

Estimates of the Risks of Cigarette Smoking

90. In order to assess the need for preventive measures it is important to attempt some quantitative estimate of the risk run by the individual who adopts or continues the smoking habit and also of the total number of deaths that may be attributed to smoking.

91. **The individual.** Three expressions of the average individual mortality risk for cigarette smokers are given in Table IV derived from some 3,000 deaths recorded by Doll and Hill[58] as occurring among 25,000 doctors observed for 8 years. Those who had given up smoking at the beginning of the period are excluded. These figures probably underestimate the risk applicable to the general population because the death rate from bronchitis among doctors is less than half that of other males in the population of England and Wales.

(i) The first expression (Table IV, 1) is a simple statement of the annual death rate from all causes per 1,000 among non-smokers and light, medium and heavy smokers, in ten year periods from the age of 35. In the first period, heavy cigarette smokers have four times the death rate of non-smokers; the difference declines to twofold by the age of 74.

(ii) The second expression is the average fractional risk of the individual man dying during each of the ten year periods between the ages of 35 and 74. The significance of these figures may be illustrated in terms of a lottery by supposing that for each ten year period the man has to draw from a box containing one marked ticket among a number of blanks. If he draws the marked ticket he dies in the next ten years. The ratios in Table IV, 2 indicate the number of tickets among which the one marked ticket is placed. Thus for a non-smoker aged 35 there is one marked ticket for the next ten years in a box of 90 tickets but for a heavy smoker of this age the marked ticket is one among only 23.

---

* The data of Doll and Hill[58] do not show any deaths from lung cancer in these groups. There is certainly some mortality which is too small to show in the size of population which they studied.

(iii) The third expression of risk is the percentage of men aged 35 who may be expected to die before the usual retiring age of 65. The chance for a non-smoker is 15% or about one in six, whereas for a heavy cigarette smoker it is 33% or one in three.

(iv) An objection to these overall mortality differences between smokers and non-smokers is that it is unlikely that all the excess deaths among smokers are due to smoking. They may in part be due to other differences between smokers and non-smokers which will not be affected by adopting or discontinuing the habit. These figures may however be taken to represent the *maximum* risk of cigarette smoking. Since it appears reasonable to assume that only a small proportion of deaths from lung cancer would have occurred in the absence of cigarette smoking, we can make some estimate of the minimum risk of cigarette smoking by presenting in Table IV, 4 and 5, death rates and risks of dying from lung cancer alone. The total risk of dying of lung cancer for a smoker of 25 or more cigarettes a day is one in fourteen between the ages of 35 and 74 and one in nine between the ages of 35 and 84.

(v) The true mortality risk attributable to smoking lies somewhere between these maximum and minimum figures. The risk of an ex-smoker who has discontinued the habit for 10 years is considerably less than that of a continuing smoker (Figures 10, p. 21 and 12, p.33).

92. **The community.** Table V lists the number of deaths that occurred in 1959 in men and women aged 30-64 from those diseases which are more frequent or severe in smokers than non-smokers. These are deaths which can be regarded as premature. If most of the lung cancer deaths are attributed to smoking and even if only a small proportion of the others are thus attributable, the total toll taken by smoking among middle aged men and women is grave. We cannot estimate suffering caused by smoking, but it must be large. Men and women prematurely disabled by bronchitis provide some of the most persistently distressed patients whom doctors are called on to attend, and many of them might well have remained healthy had they never smoked.

The Need for Preventive Measures

93. The evidence that cigarette smoking often has harmful and dangerous consequences is now so convincing that preventive measures are undoubtedly needed. Before considering what steps might be taken to modify smoking habits it is necessary to consider whether reduction of air pollution, which probably increases the incidence of both lung cancer and bronchitis (see paragraphs 32 (viii) and 49 (iii)), might make it unnecessary to take preventive action against smoking.

TABLE V

NUMBER OF DEATHS FROM COMMON DISEASES ASSOCIATED WITH SMOKING. MEN & WOMEN AGED 30-64. ENGLAND & WALES 1959

Age	Lung Cancer		Bronchitis		Coronary Heart Disease		Gastric and Duodenal Ulcer		TOTAL	
	Men	Women	Men	Women	Men	Women	Men	Women	Men	Women
30-34	54	25	26	17	138	25	17	6	235	73
35-39	170	56	49	33	476	50	40	6	735	145
40-44	391	90	116	62	853	126	69	19	1,429	297
45-49	927	186	379	113	2,017	310	118	42	3,441	651
50-54	1,958	293	924	189	3,921	706	173	53	6,976	1,241
55-59	3,232	380	1,912	357	6,087	1,509	342	81	11,573	2,327
60-64	3,549	427	2,751	657	7,194	2,831	396	113	13,890	4,028
TOTAL	10,281	1,457	6,157	1,428	20,686	5,557	1,155	320	38,279	8,762

Deaths from all causes at ages 30-64 in 1959 were 84,296 in men and 51,989 in women

94. The important benefits to health that a reduction in air pollution might confer will be considered in a later report. There are two main reasons for concluding that whatever steps are taken in this respect a reduction in cigarette smoking would prevent much suffering and many premature deaths.

(i) Studies of emigrants from Britain to countries with lower pollution-levels suggest that the effects of exposure to pollution in early life continue to raise the risks of smoking for many years[49, 64, 88]. Even if pollution were abolished completely and immediately, smokers in this country would continue to have a greater risk of lung cancer than smokers who had never been exposed to pollution. The risk could be reduced only by avoiding the smoking of cigarettes.

(ii) In countries where levels of air pollution are lower than could possibly be attained in this country in the foreseeable future, cigarette smoking is associated with a considerable increase in incidence of lung cancer and bronchitis.

95. The conclusion is that it is necessary for the health of the present population of this country that any measures which are practicable and likely to produce beneficial changes in smoking habits shall be taken promptly.

96. Although most smokers suffer no serious impairment of health or shortening of life as the result of their habit there is no certain means by which the minority who will be affected may be identified. A smoker's cough may provide a warning sign (see paragraph 120), but the adverse effects of smoking are not confined to those who cough. Full protection of the individual and the community requires preventive measures of general application.

PREVENTIVE MEASURES

Removal of Harmful Substances from Tobacco Smoke

97. **Filtration of smoke.** It is probable that all the particles in a cloud of tobacco smoke have the same chemical composition so that selective removal by filtration of particular compounds which might be specially toxic does not seem practicable. Plugs made of fine tissue paper or synthetic fibres retain a variable proportion of the smoke particles that are drawn through them. So, of course, does the un-smoked tobacco in the stub of the cigarette, more effectively, indeed, than some special filters[116, 195]. A filter plug could be made which would retain all the smoke. In practice the degree of efficiency is limited by what is acceptable to the smoker in terms of flavour and "draw resistance"; for the greater the efficiency of the filter the greater the resistance to air flow. Cigarettes with increasing filtration efficiency

48

are being introduced in the U.S.A.[205] At first they met with serious sales resistance but there is now evidence of a wider acceptance of more efficient filtration[36, 164]. In recent years there has been a great increase in sales of filter-tipped cigarettes in Britain. Present day filters have a greater filtration efficiency than the corresponding length of tobacco in a plain cigarette. About 18 % of smoke particles are retained in a cigarette stub of average length (18 mm) whereas 25% was the average retention by the filter alone from 20 representative tipped brands[215]. Comparison of the amount of smoke or tar condensed from various tipped and plain brands of cigarettes have shown that, although there is considerable variation, the average amount of condensate from the tipped brands is lower[36, 211]. Since filters vary in efficiency, it would be most desirable to have them tested by some official agency and to have the result of the test indicated on the packet so that the purchaser could distinguish a more from a less efficient filter.

98. **Modifications of tobacco.** Some strains of the tobacco plant have a low nicotine content and the nicotine content of ordinary tobaccos can be reduced by a variety of methods. The use of such tobaccos is of uncertain value, since it is not known what part nicotine plays in the hazards of cigarette smoking. Such low nicotine tobaccos might however be worthy of trial in patients with peptic ulcer or arterial diseases who fail to give up smoking. At present no brands of cigarettes on sale in Britain have a specially reduced nicotine content. Such cigarettes are marketed in the U.S.A., but without any regulation concerning the meaning of the term "denicotinised."

99. The tar and thus, possibly, the carcinogenic content of tobacco smoke can also be reduced by various methods of treatment of the tobacco[199]. If cigarettes producing smoke with a reduced tar content were to be marketed, some official procedure for testing the cigarette and marking the packets would be desirable as in the case of filter-tipped cigarettes.

100. It should be realised that since we cannot identify the substances in tobacco smoke that may be injurious to health, no firm claims for the safety of modified cigarette tobaccos or filters can be made. It would, of course, be many years before it would be possible to detect any effect upon death rates resulting from the use of cigarettes with filter tips, or of modified tobaccos. A reduction in the prevalence of smoker's cough among those who had used such cigarettes or tobaccos might give early evidence of a beneficial effect.

Adoption of Safer Smoking Habits

101. The unburnt part of a cigarette acts as a filter so that as the cigarette burns down, smoke condensed in the second part is redistilled. Thus the smoke from the second half contains a higher and

49

steadily rising concentration of potentially toxic substance than the smoke of the first half. Some means of persuading cigarette smokers to stub out their cigarettes before the second half was burnt would almost certainly reduce the risk. This might be more practicable for confirmed smokers than complete abandonment of the habit.

102. Since pipe and cigar smokers have a smaller risk than cigarette smokers of developing lung cancer, bronchitis and coronary heart disease, the possibility that cigarette smokers could be persuaded to change to these safer forms of smoking must be considered. A combination of education and fiscal measures might achieve some measure of success in this respect.

Discouragement of Smoking

103. There can, of course, be no question of prohibiting a habit which most smokers enjoy without injury to their health, but the amount of ill-health and shortening of life that is attributable to smoking is now so great that means must be sought to reduce the vast and increasing prevalence of the habit. At present both social custom and commercial pressure outbid the voice of caution and the balance must be redressed.

104. **Measures directed to adolescents or young adults.** Whatever may be the attitude of present smokers in balancing their enjoyment and dependence on the habit against the risks involved, there is no doubt of our responsibility to protect the coming generation from developing the same dependence. The problem of prevention is thus primarily one of education and social action directed to children, adolescents and young adults who have not yet formed fixed smoking habits.

105. Although anti-smoking education by means of lectures, pamphlets or posters has been introduced into many schools in Britain this has hitherto been done only on a small scale. One study[107] of the effects of a poster display, a talk by the headmaster, a 40-minute discussion group on the dangers of smoking and the showing of two films concerned with lung cancer and smoking, to children in the third year at a secondary modern school had a small but measurable effect on the smoking habits of the boys but not of the girls when compared with habits of children in a neighbouring school. A more elaborate experiment was carried out in Portland, Oregon[103]. Here the schoolchildren were divided into six groups, one acting as a control. Attempts were made to dissuade the others from taking up smoking in five different ways during a period of eight months, as follows:—

(a) *Contemporary:* emphasis on immediate disadvantages of smoking, e.g. social, financial, athletic, etc.

(b) *Remote:* emphasis on the relationship of smoking to lung cancer.

(c) *Both-sided:* as in (a) and (b) but more permissive, admitting the social advantages as well as the medical disadvantages of smoking.

(d) *Authoritative.*

(e) *Adult role taking:* suggesting that the school children should inform their parents and families of the dangers of smoking.

Among the control boys the "recruitment rate" of non-smokers to smoking (i.e. percentage of non-smokers who started smoking during the eight months of the study) was 13%. A significant reduction (to 7·7%) was produced by the "remote" approach and a nearly significant reduction (to 9%) was produced by the "both-sided" approach. The others had no effect. Among the control girls the recruitment rate was 6·4%. It was significantly reduced (to 2%) in the first two groups and in the "both-sided" group (to 3·4%). There was no reduction in the other two groups. This experiment suggests that appropriate education can dissuade a significant proportion of children from starting to smoke.

106. A high proportion of children in Britain are aware that smoking can impair health[18, 28], and about half of them have heard of the connection between smoking and lung cancer. A remote belief is, however, very different from real acceptance of a risk as being important to the individual. Far more effort needs to be expended on educating children about the risks of smoking, with careful assessment of the effect of different forms of instruction. Only in this way will it be possible to discover what are the most effective methods. Any change that might be brought about in the smoking habits of adults would almost certainly be reflected in a consequent change in adolescent smoking since there is a definite association between the smoking habits of parents and their children. This might be the most important consequence of a reduction in smoking by adults.

107. The recent trend of cigarette advertising to appeal to the younger members of the community has been noted (paragraph 10). Although there is no direct evidence that advertising initiates and perpetuates the smoking habit in young people, there can be no doubt that any effect this trend might have would be harmful, and it should be halted.

108. **Measures directed to adults.** In the last ten years the connection between smoking and cancer of the lung and other diseases has been widely referred to in the press, and in sound and television broadcasts. In a recent survey in Edinburgh almost every member of the community had heard of this connection[27a]. Only one-third, however, definitely accepted the evidence that cigarette smoking could lead to lung cancer. Twice as many smokers (23%) as non-smokers

(11%) definitely disagreed with this idea. There is clearly room for more persistent public education in this matter. A large majority of smokers were, however, aware of a variety of other health hazards of smoking and yet of those smokers (about two-fifths) who expressed a desire to stop smoking only 3% mentioned a fear of cancer and only a quarter mentioned other health hazards as their reasons. Expense was given as their reason by two-thirds of those wishing to discontinue. It might therefore be thought that campaigns drawing attention to the hazards and disadvantages of smoking would fail to deter more than an insignificant minority of steady or heavy smokers from continuing the habit. Indeed, a recent vigorous campaign in Edinburgh over a period of one year had no effect in changing adult smoking habits nor in changing the proportion of the public who believed that smoking might cause cancer of the lung[27]. More than mere information is required. Many smokers regard the lack of any official action against cigarette smoking as an indication that the evidence is at present "only theoretical" or "mere statistics". If the Government do not consider it necessary to take action, it is argued, no action is as yet required of the individual. The contrast between the smoking habits of doctors and the general public (Figure 4, p. 9) is notable in this matter. Doctors are in a position not only to read and appreciate the scientific evidence on the hazards of cigarette smoking but also in their daily practice they witness the tragic consequences of the habit.

109. It is therefore necessary that any campaign to increase public information concerning the hazards of smoking must be reinforced by some evidence of active concern by the Government. Government action hitherto has been confined to statements to Parliament by the Minister of Health. In February 1954[146], he stated that he accepted the view of his Standing Advisory Committee on Cancer and Radiotherapy that there was a strong presumption that the relationship between cancer of the lung and smoking was causal. On that occasion he publicised the matter by a press conference. In July 1957[147], the Minister stated that the Government's response to the advice of the Medical Research Council that smoking played a major part in the increase of deaths from lung cancer was "that the facts should be made known to all those with responsibility for health education". Local health authorities were asked to take appropriate steps to inform the general public and in this task they would have the assistance of the Central and Scottish Councils for Health Education.

110. There is little evidence of any steps having been taken, apart from the attempts to educate schoolchildren to which reference has been made (paragraph 105). The Central Council for Health Education have prepared some valuable pamphlets and provided lecturers to

speak on the health aspects of smoking. In the years 1958-59 they spent £1,150 on these activities. Local authorities purchased from the Central Council material for health education in relation to smoking amounting to £3,424 in the years 1956-59. These figures may be compared with the sum of £27,000,000 spent by the tobacco industry in advertising their goods in the same four years. In 1960 the local authorities spent a further £200 with the Central Council and the tobacco manufacturers spent £11,000,000. There is, moreover, some resistance to the efforts of the Central Council for Health Education. A poster was devised in 1958 showing the smoke issuing from a cigarette spelling the word "Cancer", but local bill-posting contractors on the advice of the British Poster Advertising Association, declined to carry out the work of display. The reason given was that the Joint Censorship Committee of the poster advertising industry considered that the inference from the poster was that one cigarette could cause cancer and this was misleading to the public[45a].

111. In December 1960 the Minister of Health[148], in answer to a question about campaigns aimed at discouraging young people from smoking, said: "There is good evidence that people in Britain are widely aware of the risks involved in smoking. The health education measures of local authorities are largely directed to the young and should ensure that this awareness is maintained and intensified". Since 1957, tobacco consumption and particularly cigarette smoking have continued to increase, and recent evidence of the wide prevalence of smoking among schoolchildren does not suggest that such education as is being carried out is having much effect.

POSSIBLE ACTION BY THE GOVERNMENT

112. Some decisive steps should be taken by the Government to curb the present rising consumption of tobacco, and especially of cigarettes. This action could be taken along the following lines:—

113. **Public education.** Much more imagination, effort and money should be devoted to drawing the attention of the public to the hazards of smoking. Special attention should be paid to effective education of schoolchildren, but use should also be made of every modern method of advertising, including posters, press notices and short items on radio and television. The attention of parents should continually be drawn to their responsibility for dissuading and discouraging their children from smoking. Such public education might also advise safer smoking habits for those whose addiction is too strong to be broken. Appropriate surveys of smoking habits should be organised periodically to ensure that accurate information about the effects of

education by various means, especially of schoolchildren, is obtained in order to discover and implement the most effective of them.

114. An educational campaign among children might be supported by *more effective restrictions on the sale of tobacco* to children. The regulation forbidding the sale of tobacco to children under the age of 16 is widely flouted and, in any case, cigarettes are freely available in slot machines.

115. **Restriction of advertisement of tobacco.** Any increase in public education concerning the risk of smoking would at present be in conflict with the vast expenditure on advertising tobacco. While it may be doubted whether advertisement does much to initiate the smoking habit, and it is predominantly designed to attract smokers towards the advertiser's particular brand rather than to increase overall consumption (Appendix 1), legislation to prevent or at least to restrict the advertisement of a habit which causes such widespread injury to health would be reasonable and would provide evidence of official acceptance of the reality of the hazard. There are a number of precedents for legislation to control advertising in the interest of public health.

116. **Wider restriction of smoking in public places.** This would be desirable for the convenience and enjoyment of what may be an increasing number of non-smokers and it might ultimately contribute much to the discontinuance of smoking by altering social acceptance of the habit.

117. **Taxation.** Since financial considerations are those most commonly advanced by smokers as their reason for regretting the habit, it might be thought that increases in tobacco taxation would persuade many smokers to stop. There was, indeed, a sharp fall in cigarette consumption after the large increase of taxation on tobacco imposed in 1947, but this was followed by a steady rise (Figure 1, p. 3). It seems unlikely that increased taxation would have any lasting deterrent effect. A differential increase in taxation of cigarettes with a reduction of taxation on pipe and cigar tobacco might, however, persuade many cigarette smokers who cannot forsake the habit to change to safer forms of smoking. The example of the Scandinavian countries is relevant to this point. For many years cigar smoking has been more popular and cigarette smoking less popular in these countries than in Britain, and this may be an important reason for their lower mortality from lung cancer and bronchitis[32, 154].

118. **Smoke analyses on cigarette packets.** Since there is reason to assume that the harmful effects of cigarette smoking may be due to tar, volatile irritants and nicotine in the smoke, regulations might be introduced whereby the purchaser of any brand of cigarettes could discover the average amount of these substances produced by one of

these cigarettes under standard smoking conditions. The figure might be established by an official testing agency and stamped on the packet. This figure would have to be expressed as yield per gram of cigarette to allow for different sizes of cigarettes. One objection to this might be the varying yield obtained from the same brand when tested at different times, but this could be overcome by quoting the average yield of a series of samples of the brand, or by insisting that manufacturers should not vary the type of tobacco they incorporate in their cigarettes. Such analyses are regularly published in the U.S.A. but not by an official agency[36]. No claim should be made that any particular brand of cigarette was safer than any other (see para. 100).

119. **Anti-smoking clinics.** The Ministry of Health through the National Health Service might consider the organisation of experimental anti-smoking clinics to be held in hospitals and chest clinics throughout the country. To these clinics doctors might refer people who were finding difficulty in forsaking smoking. Here they could receive expert advice and also the assistance of other people who had succeeded in freeing themselves from addiction to tobacco. Such clinics have been started in Sweden and are reported to be meeting with some success[68]. There is some evidence that a buffered lobeline tablet[9, 167] or even nicotine injections[109] may provide some satisfaction during the period of withdrawal symptoms, and controlled trials have shown that patients assisted by lobeline may be more successful in stopping smoking than patients given dummy tablets. Further trials of this and other methods of assisting people to free themselves from the smoking habit might be carried out in clinics of this kind.

DOCTORS AND THEIR PATIENTS

120. Patients with bronchitis, peptic ulcer, and arterial disease should be advised to stop smoking. Despite the manifest disadvantages of smoking to these patients many of them continue the habit. It may often be noted that these patients have not been given really firm advice by their doctors about the need to stop smoking. The question of the significance of a "smoker's cough" is one which requires further investigation. There is evidence of an association between chronic bronchitis and cancer of the lung[29, 169, 176]. The pathological changes found in the bronchi of heavy smokers are thought by some authorities to be precancerous and are such as would be expected to cause chronic cough and expectoration. There is little doubt that smokers who have a productive cough have an increased risk of developing disabling bronchitis and they may also have an increased risk of lung cancer[117, 200]. Even a simple smoker's cough may thus be an indication that the habit must be given up.

121. This report has presented extensive evidence of the hazards of cigarette smoking. The doctor who smokes cigarettes must, like any other individual, balance these risks against the pleasures he derives from smoking and make his choice, but he has a special responsibility because of the effect that his choice has upon all those with whom he comes into social and professional contact. The doctor who smokes will inevitably lessen the effect of any campaign of public education concerning the consequence of the habit and will find it harder to help his patients who need to stop smoking.

The Committee to report on Smoking and Atmospheric Pollution was approved by the College in April 1959, with the following terms of reference:—

"To report on the question of smoking and atmospheric pollution in relation to carcinoma of the lung and other illnesses."

The composition of the Committee is as follows:—

The President, Sir Robert Platt, Bt.
Sir Aubrey Lewis
Dr. J. G. Scadding
Dr. R. Bodley Scott
Dr. F. Avery Jones
Dr. N. C. Oswald
Dr. C. M. Fletcher, *Hon. Secretary*
Dr. J. N. Morris
Dr. J. A. Scott

This report was presented to the general meeting of Fellows of the College on October 26th, 1961 and approved for publication.

APPENDIX 1

The notes given below were sent to the Royal College of Physicians Committee on Smoking and Air Pollution by the Tobacco Advisory Committee with the figures they provided on expenditure on advertising of tobacco goods in recent years. The Committee consider it appropriate that the Manufacturers' views should be made known but wish to make it clear that they are not, of course, endorsed.

1. Press and television advertising expenditure on tobacco goods in the U.K. in 1959 was 0·52% of retail expenditure on these goods whereas press and television advertising expenditure on all consumer goods and services was 0·87% of retail expenditure on all consumer goods and services. Press and television advertising expenditure on tobacco goods could thus be increased by two-thirds without exceeding the proportion that press and television advertising expenditure on consumer goods and services generally bears to public expenditure on these goods and services.

2. Advertising of tobacco products takes the form of advertising of individual brands. There is no direct appeal to non-smokers to smoke as there is, for example, to non-milk drinkers to drink a pint of milk a day or to bareheaded men to wear a hat. The purpose of brand advertising is simply to sell the brand advertised, which primarily means to sell that brand at the expense of competing brands.

3. The tobacco manufacturers in this country have never encouraged excessive smoking. There has never been any advertising in which smokers have been urged to smoke *more*.

4. The effect of brand advertising on total consumption is likely to have been small, as may be seen from the fact that the consumption of pipe tobaccos, cigars and snuff has declined continuously since 1900 despite very considerable advertising expenditure.

5. As already explained to the Committee, in the years following the war, cigarettes and tobacco (especially cigarettes) were in short supply because of the scarcity of leaf tobacco. In these conditions—under which manufacturers could meet only a proportion of the demand for their goods—

advertising expenditure was at a relatively low level and remained so until 1954 when supplies of leaf became more plentiful.

6. In 1937/38, press advertising expenditure on cigarettes was 81% of total press advertising expenditure on tobacco goods. In 1958/59, press and television advertising expenditure on cigarettes was 82% of total press and television advertising expenditure on tobacco goods. On the other hand, cigarettes have increased from 77% of the total weight of tobacco smoked in 1937/38 to 86% in 1958/59.

7. It has been alleged that advertising of competitive brands involves unnecessary duplication of expenditure. In a competitive economy, however, competitive advertising is a corollary to competitive manufacture, and is an integral part of the cost of distribution. Competition however ensures that the manufacturer keeps all costs, including those of advertising, to a minimum.

8. Although the law permits young persons over the age of 16 to purchase cigarettes it can not be said that any manufacturer in this country has brought a disproportionate weight of advertising to bear on this class of consumer.

9. The tobacco manufacturers have never encouraged smoking by schoolchildren and have never in the slightest degree aimed advertising at them. No attempt, for example, has been made to secure advertising space for tobacco goods in boys' and girls' papers or to advertise cigarettes in the breaks in children's television programmes. Further, the manufacturers discourage the sale of cigarettes singly which would facilitate smoking by schoolchildren. The sale of cigarettes to children for their own use through automatic vending machines is negligible and it is illegal for the shopkeeper knowingly to allow these sales.

APPENDIX 2

The figures concerning filtration efficiency in para. 97 have been supplied by the Tobacco Manufacturers' Standing Committee, who have at the same time pointed out that in their view the particulate phase retention efficiency of a filter plug does not give any indication of the relevance of a filter plug to the health problem.

REFERENCES

1. ABRAHAM, K. (1927): *Selected Papers*. London: Hogarth Press, p. 270.
2. AMERICAN HEART ASSOCIATION (1960): Cigarette smoking and cardio-vascular diseases. Circulation, **22**, 160.
3. ASHFORD, J. R., BROWN, S., DUFFIELD, D. P., SMITH, C. S. and FAY, J. W. J. (1961): The relation between smoking habits and physique, respiratory symptoms, ventilatory function and radiological pneumoconiosis. Brit. J. prev. soc. Med. **15**, 106.
4. ATTINGER, E. C., GOLDSTEIN, M. M., and SEGAL, M. S. (1957): The effects of smoking on the mechanics of breathing. (1) In normal subjects, (2) In patients with cardio-pulmonary disease. Amer. Rev. resp. Dis., **77**, 1 and 10.
5. AUERBACH, O., GERE, J. B., FORMAN, J. B., PETRICK, T. G., SMOLIN, H. J., MUEHSAM, G. E., KASSOUNY, D. J., and STOUT, A. P. (1957): Changes in the bronchial epithelium in relation to smoking and cancer of the lung. New Engl. J. Med., **256**, 97.
6. AUERBACH, O., STOUT, A. P., HAMMOND, E. C. and GARFINKEL, L. (1961): Changes in bronchial epithelium in relation to cigarette smoking and in relation to lung cancer. Ibid. **265**, 253.

7. BALLENGER, J. J. (1960): Experimental effect of cigarette smoke on human respiratory cilia. New England J. Med., **263**, 832.
8. BARGERON, JR., L. M., EHMKE, D., GONLUBOL, F., CASTELLANOS, A., SIEGEL, A. and BING, R. J. (1957): Effect of cigarette smoking on coronary blood flow and myocardial metabolism. Circulation **15**, 251.
9. BARTLETT, W. A., and WHITEHEAD, R. W. (1957): The effectiveness of meprobamate and lobeline as smoking deterrents. J. Lab. clin. Med., **50**, 278.
10. BATTERMAN, R. C. (1955): Gastro-intestinal tract. In *The Biologic effects of tobacco*. Edited by E. L. Wynder and J. Garland. Little, Brown and Co., Boston.
11. BATTERMAN, R. C. and EHRENFELD, I. (1949): The influence of smoking upon the management of the peptic ulcer patient. Gastroenterology, **12**, 575.
12. BENTLEY, H. R. and BERRY, E. G. N. (1959): *The constituents of tobacco smoke*. An annotated bibliography. Tobacco Manuf. Stand. Comm. Res. Papers. No. 3 and supplement No. 1 (1960).

13. BERKSON, J. (1958): Smoking and lung cancer. Some observations on two recent reports. J. Amer. Stat. Ass., **53**, 28.
14. BERKSON, J. (1959): The statistical investigation of smoking and cancer of the lung. Proc. Mayo Clin., **34**, 206.
15. BERKSON, J. (1960): Smoking and cancer of the lung. Proc. Mayo Clin., **35**, 367.
16. BEST, E. W. R., JOSIE, G. H., and WALKER, C. B. (1960): A Canadian study of mortality in relation to smoking habits. A preliminary report. Canad. J. Publ. Hlth., **52**, 99.
17. BLACKBURN, H., BROZEK, J. and TAYLOR, H. L. (1959): Lung volume in smokers and non-smokers. Ann. intern. Med., **51**, 68.
18. BOTHWELL, P. W. (1959): The epidemiology of cigarette smoking in rural school children. Med. Offr., **102**, 125.
19. BRESLOW, L., HOAGLIN, L., RASMUSSEN, G. and ABRAMS, H. K. (1954): Occupation and cigarette smoking as factors in lung cancer. Amer. J. Publ. Hlth., **44**, 171.
20. BROZEK, J. and KEYS, A. (1957): Changes of body weight in normal men who stop smoking cigarettes. Science, **125**, 1203.
21. BUECHLEY, R. W., DRAKE, R. M., and BRESLOW, L. (1958): Relationship of amount of cigarette smoking to coronary heart disease mortality rates in men. Circulation, **18**, 1085.
22. BURN, J. H. (1961): The action of nicotine and the pleasure of smoking. Advanc. Sci. Lond., **17**, 494.
23. BURN, J. H. and RAND, M. J., (1958): Action of nicotine on the heart. Brit. med. J., **i**, 137.
24. BURN, J. H., TRUELOVE, L. H., and BURN, I. H. (1945): The antidiuretic action of nicotine and smoking. Brit. med. J., **i**, 403.
25. BURNEY, L. E. (1959): Smoking and lung cancer. A statement of the Public Health Service. J. Amer. med. Ass., **171**, 1829.

26. CARTWRIGHT, A., MARTIN, F. M., and THOMSON, J. G. (1959): Distribution and development of smoking habits. Lancet, **2**, 725.
27. CARTWRIGHT, A., MARTIN, F. M. and THOMSON, J. G. (1960): Efficacy of an anti-smoking campaign. Lancet, **i**, 327.
27a. CARTWRIGHT, A., MARTIN, F. M. and THOMSON, J. G. (1960): Health hazards of cigarette smoking, current popular beliefs. Brit. J. prev. soc. Med., **14**, 160.
28. CARTWRIGHT, A., THOMSON, J. G., and a group of Edinburgh D.P.H. students (1960): Young smokers. An attitude study among school children, touching also on parental influence. Brit. J. prev. soc. Med., **14**, 28.
29. CASE, R. A. M., and LEA, A. J. (1955): Mustard gas poisoning, chronic bronchitis and lung cancer. Brit. J. prev. soc. Med., **9**, 62.
30. CHANG, S. C. (1957): Microscopic properties of whole mounts and sections of human bronchial epithelium of smokers and non-smokers. Cancer, Philad., **10**, 1246.
31. CHARLES, J. (1955): The Contrivance of Collegiation. Lancet, **ii**, 987.
32. CHRISTENSEN, O. W. and WOOD, C. H. (1958): Bronchitis mortality rates in England and in Denmark. Brit. med. J., **i**, 621.

33. CLAPARIDE, E. and ISRAILOVITCH, D (1902): Influence du tabac sur l'association des idees. C. R. Soc. Biol., (Paris), **54,** 758.
34. CLEMO, G. R. (1959): Symposium on atmospheric pollution, (a) Some aspects of the chemistry of cigarette smoke and its possible implications. R. Soc. Health J., Lond. **79,** 74.
35. COLLEGE OF GENERAL PRACTITIONERS (1961): Chronic bronchitis in Great Britain. A national survey carried out by the respiratory disease study group of the College of General Practitioners. Brit. med. J., **ii,** 973.
36. CONSUMER UNION (1961): Cigarettes. Consumer Reports, **26,** 203.
37. COOK, J. W. (1957): Chemical carcinogens and their significance. Lancet, **i,** 333.
38. COOPER, P., HARROWER, H. W., STEIN, H. L., and MOORE, G. F. (1958): The effect of cigarette smoking on intragastric balloon pressure and temperature of patients with duodenal ulcer. Gastroenterology, **35,** 176.
39. COOPER, R. L., GILBERT, J. A. S., and LINDSEY, A. J. (1955): Polycyclic hydrocarbons in cigarette smoke. The contribution made by the paper. Brit. J. Cancer, **9,** 442.
40. COOPER, R. L. and LINDSEY, A. J. (1955): 3 : 4-6 benzpyrene and other polycyclic hydro-carbons in cigarette smoke. Brit. J. Cancer, **9,** 304.
41. CORNFIELD, J., HAENSZEL, W., HAMMOND, E. C., LILIENFELD. A. M., SHIMKIN, M. B., and WYNDER, E. L. (1959): Smoking and lung cancer. Recent evidence and a discussion of some questions. J. nat. Cancer Inst., **22,** 173.

42. DAFF, M. E. and KENNAWAY, E. L. (1950): The arsenic content of tobacco and of tobacco smoke. Brit. J. Cancer, **4,** 173.
43. DAFF, M. E., DOLL, R., and KENNAWAY, E. L. (1951): Cancer of the lung in relation to tobacco. Brit. J. Cancer, **5,** 1.
44. DALHAMN, T. (1956): The effect of cigarette smoke on ciliary activity in the upper respiratory tract. A.M.A. Arch. Otolaryng. **70,** 166.
45. DALY, C. (1959): Air pollution and causes of death. Brit. J. prev. soc. Med. **13,** 14.
45a. DALZELL-WARD, A. J. (1961): Personal communication.
46. DAVIES, C. N. (1957): Dangers of cigarette smoking (letter). Brit. med. J., **ii,** 410.
47. DAVIES, D. F. (1960): Review of the evidence on a relationship between smoking and lung cancer. J. Chron. Dis. **11,** 579.
48. DAWBER, T. R., KANNEL, W. B., REVOTSKIE, N., STOKES, J., KAGAN, A., and GORDON, T. (1959): Some factors associated with the development of coronary heart disease. Amer. J. publ. Hlth. **49,** 1349.
49. DEAN, G. (1959): Lung cancer among white South Africans. Brit. med. J., **ii,** 852. And (1961) ibid. **ii,** 1599.
50. DOLL, W. R. (1953): Bronchial carcinoma; Incidence and aetiology. Brit. med. J., **ii,** 521.
51. DOLL, W. R. (1958): In *Carcinoma of the Lung* edited by J. R. Bignall. Livingstone, London.
52. DOLL, W. R. (1959): Occupational lung cancer; a review. Brit. J. industr. Med. **16,** 181.

53. DOLL, W. R. (1959): Lung cancer and cigarette smoking. Acta Union Internationale contre le Cancer, 15, 417.
54. DOLL, W. R. and HILL, A. B. (1950): Smoking and carcinoma of the lung. Brit. med. J., ii, 739.
55. DOLL, W. R. and HILL, A. B. (1952): A study of the aetiology of carcinoma of the lung. Brit. med. J., ii, 1271.
56. DOLL, W. R. and HILL, A. B. (1954): The mortality of doctors in relation to their smoking habits. A preliminary report. Brit. med. J., i, 1451.
57. DOLL, W. R. and HILL, A. B. (1956): Lung cancer and other causes of death in relation to smoking. A second report on the mortality of British doctors. Brit. med. J., ii, 1071.
58. DOLL, W. R. and HILL, A. B. (1961): Personal communication.
59. DOLL, W. R., HILL, A. B., GRAY, P. G., and PARR, E. A. (1959): Lung cancer mortality and the length of cigarette ends. Brit. med. J., i, 322.
60. DOLL, W. R., HILL, A. B., and KREYBERG, L. (1957): The significance of cell type in relation to the aetiology of lung cancer. Brit. J. Cancer, 11, 43.
61. DOLL, W. R., JONES, F. A., and PYGOTT, F. (1958): Effect of smoking on production and maintenance of gastric and duodenal ulcer. Lancet, i, 657.
62. DORN, H. F. (1959): Tobacco consumption and mortality from cancer and other diseases. U.S. Publ. Hlth. Rep., 74, 581.
63. DUUREN, B. L. VAN (1958): Identification of some polynuclear aromatic hydrocarbons in cigarette smoke condensate. J. nat. Cancer Inst., 21, 1.

64. EASTCOTT, D. F. (1956): The epidemiology of lung cancer in New Zealand. Lancet, i, 37.
65. EDWARDS, J. H. (1957): Contribution of cigarette smoking to respiratory disease. Brit. J. prev. soc. Med., 11, 10.
66. EDWARDS, F., MCKEOWN, T., and WHITFIELD, A. G. W. (1959): Association between smoking and disease in men over sixty. Lancet, i, 196.
67. EICH, R. H., GILBERT, R. and AUCHINCLOSS, J. H. (1956): Effects of smoking on respiratory mechanics in chronic pulmonary emphysema. Clin. Res. Proc., 4, 151.
68. EJRUP, B. (1961): Proposals for treatment of smokers with severe clinical symptoms brought about by their smoking habits. British Columbia Med. J., 2, 441.
69. ENGELBRETH-HOLM, J. and AHLMANN, J. (1957): Production of carcinoma in ST/Eh mice with cigarette tar. Acta path. microbiol. Scand., 41, 267.
70. EYSENCK, H. J., TARRANT, M., WOOLF, M. and ENGLAND, L. (1960): Smoking and personality. Brit. med. J., i, 1456.

71. FAIRBAIRN, A. S. and Reid, D. D. (1958): Air pollution and other local factors in respiratory disease. Brit. J. prev. soc. Med., 12, 94.
72. FENICHEL, O. (1954): Collected papers. First series. London: Routledge and Kegan Paul, p. 233.
73. FISHER, R. A. (1957): Dangers of cigarette smoking (letter). Brit. med. J., ii, 297.

74. FISHER, R. A. (1958): Lung cancer and cigarettes. Nature, **182,** 108 and 596.
75. FISHER, R. A. (1959): *Smoking: the Cancer Controversy.* Edinburgh: Oliver and Boyd.
76. FLETCHER, C. M. (1959): Chronic bronchitis: its prevalence, nature and pathogenesis. Amer. Rev. resp. Dis., **80,** 483.
77. FLETCHER, C. M. (1961): Chronic bronchitis, smoking and air pollution. *Proceedings of conference on Smoking and Health.* Charles C. Thomas, Illinois. (In the press).
78. FLETCHER, C. M., and TINKER, C. M. (1961): Chronic bronchitis: a further study of simple diagnostic methods in a working population. Brit. med. J., **i,** 1491.
79. FLICK, A. L., and PATON, R. R. (1959): Obstructive emphysema in cigarette smokers. Arch. intern. Med., **104,** 518.
79a. FRAZIER, T. M., DAVIS, G. H., GOLSTEIN, H. and GOLDBERG, I. D. (1961): Cigarette smoking and prematurity: a prospective study. Amer. J. Obst. Gyn., **81,** 988.
80. FREUD, S. (1949): *Three essays on the theory of sexuality.* Trans. J. Strachey. London: Imago.
81. FRIBERG, L., KAIJ, L., DENCKER, S. J., and JONSSON, E. (1959): Smoking habits of monozygotic and dizygotic twins. Brit. med. J., **i,** 1090.

82. GELLHORN, A. (1958): The co-carcinogenic activity of cigarette tobacco tar. Cancer Res., **18,** 510.
83. GELLHORN, A., KLAUSNER, C., and HIBBERT, J. (1956): Co-carcinogenicity of cigarette tobacco tar. Proc. Amer. Ass. Cancer Res., **2,** 109.
84. GOFMAN, J. W., LINDGREN, F. T., STRISOWER, B., LALLA, O. DE, GLAZIER, F. and TAMPLIN, A. (1955): Cigarette smoking, serum lipoproteins, and coronary heart disease. Geriatrics, **10,** 349.
85. GRAY, I. (1929): Gastric response to tobacco smoking. Ann. intern. Med., **3,** 267.
86. GREENBERG, L. A., LESTER, D., and HAGGARD, H. W. (1952): The absorption of nicotine in tobacco smoking. J. Pharmacol. Exper. Therap. **104,** 162.
87. GWYNN, R. H., and SALAMAN, M. H. (1954): Studies on promotion of tumour development (co-carcinogenesis). A. R. Brit. Emp. Canc. Campgn., **32,** 171.

88. HAENSZEL, W. (1961): Quantitative evaluation of etiologic factors in lung cancer. In *Proceedings of conference on Tobacco and Health.* Charles C. Thomas, Illinois. (In the press) and J. Nat. Cancer Inst., **26,** 37.
89. HAENSZEL, W., SHIMKIN, M. B., and MILLER, H. P. (1956): Tobacco smoking patterns in the United States. U.S. Public Health Monograph No. 45. Washington.
90. HAMER, D. and WOODHOUSE, D. L. (1956): Biological tests for carcinogenic action of tar from cigarette smoke. Brit. J. Cancer, **10,** 49.
91. HAMMOND, E. C. (1958): Lung cancer death rates in England and Wales compared with those in the U.S.A. Brit. med. J., **ii,** 649.

92. HAMMOND, E. C. (1959): Inhalation in relation to type and amount of smoking. J. Amer. Statis. Ass., **54**, 35.

93. HAMMOND, E. C. (1960): Smoking in relation to heart disease. Amer. J. Publ. Hlth., **50**, No. 3., Part II, 20.

94. HAMMOND, E. C. and HORN, D. (1958): Smoking and death rates—report on forty-four months of follow-up of 187,783 men. Part 1 (total mortality), Part 2 (death rates by cause). J. Amer. med. Ass., **166**, 1159 and 1294.

95. HEATH, C. W. (1958): Differences between smokers and non-smokers. A.M.A., Arch. int. Med., **101**, 377.

96. HEATON, J. M., MCCORMICK, A. J. A. and FREEMAN, A. G. (1958): Tobacco amblyopia. A clinical manifestation of vitamin-B12 deficiency. Lancet, **ii**, 286.

97. HELLPACH, W. H. (1949): *Klinische Psychologie.* Stuttgart.

98. HERDAN, G. (1958): The increase in the mortality due to cancer of the lung in the light of the distribution of the disease among the different social classes and occupations. Brit. J. Cancer, **12**, 492.

99. HIGGINS, I. T. T. (1959): Tobacco smoking, respiratory symptoms and ventilatory capacity. Studies in random samples of the population. Brit. med. J., **i**, 325.

100. HILDING, A. C. (1956): On cigarette smoking, bronchial carcinoma and ciliary action. II. Experimental study on the filtering action of cows' lungs, the deposition of tar in the bronchial tree and removal by ciliary action. New Engl. J. Med., **254**, 1155.

101. HILL, A. B., and DOLL, W. R. (1960): Deaths from lung cancer (letter). Lancet, **i**, 1292.

102. HOFSTAETTER, R. (1934): Ueber das Abgewohnen des Rauchens. Wien, med. W'schr., **84**, 95.

103. HORN, D. (1960): Modifying smoking habits in high school students. Children, **7**, 63.

104. HORN, D., COURTS, F. A., TAYLOR, R. M., and SOLOMON, E. S. (1959): Cigarette smoking among high school students. Amer. J. publ. Hlth., **49**, 1497.

105. HUEPER, W. C. (1956): Environmental causes of cancer of the lung other than tobacco smoke. Dis. Chest., **30**, 141.

106. IDE, G., SUNTZEFF, V., and COWDRY, E. V. (1959): Comparison of the histopathology of tracheal and bronchial epithelium of smokers and non-smokers. Cancer, **12**, 473.

107. JEFFERYS, M., and WESTAWAY, W. R. (1961): Catch them before they start: A report on an attempt to influence children's smoking habits. Hlth. Educ. J., **19**, 3.

108. JOHNSTON, L. M. (1942): Tobacco smoking and nicotine. Lancet, **ii**, 742.

109. JOHNSTON, L. M. (1952): Cure of tobacco smoking. Lancet, **ii**, 480.

110. JOHNSTONE, R. A. W., and PLYMMER, J. R. (1959): The chemical constituents of tobacco and tobacco smoke. Chem. Rev., **59**, 885.

111. KAHLER, H., and LLOYD, B. J. (1957): The electron microscopy of tobacco smoke. J. nat. Cancer Inst., **18**, 217.

112. KARPOVICH, P. V., and HALE, C. J. (1951): Tobacco smoking and physical performance. J. appl. Physiol., **3**, 616.

113. KARVONEN, M., ORMA, E., KEYS, A., FIDANZA, F., and BROZEK, J. (1959): Cigarette smoking, serum-cholesterol, blood pressure and body fatness. Lancet, **i**, 492.

114. KENNAWAY, E., and LINDSEY, A. J. (1958): Some possible exogenous factors in the causation of lung cancer. Brit. med. Bull., **14**, 124.

115. KISSEN, D. M. (1960): Psycho-social factors in cigarette smoking motivation. Med. Offr, **104**, 365.

116. KOSAK, A. I. (1955): Chemistry. In *The Biologic Effects of Tobacco*. Ed. Wynder and J. Garland. Little, Brown and Co., Boston.

117. KONLUMIES, M. (1953): Smoking and pulmonary carcinoma. Acta radiol. Stockh., **39**, 255.

118. LAM, J. (1955): Measuring temperature during combustion in cigarettes, cigarillos, cigars and pipes. Acta path. et microbiol. Scand., **36**, 503.

119. LANGER, G., and FISHER, M. A. (1956): Concentration and particle size of cigarette smoke particles. A.M.A. Arch. Indust. Hlth., **13**, 372.

120. LARSON, P. S., HAAG, H. B., and SILVETTE, H. (1961): *Tobacco—experimental and clinical studies. A comprehensive account of the world literature.* Balliere, Tindall & Cox, London.

123. IBID: pp. 4-5.

124. IBID: pp. 107-110.

125. IBID: pp. 203-206.

126. IBID: pp. 613-618.

127. IBID: pp. 677-683.

128. IBID: pp. 732-734.

129. LAWTON, M. P. and GOLDMAN, A. E. (1958): Cigarette smoking and attitudes towards the aetiology of lung cancer. Amer. Psychologist, **13**, 342 (Abstract).

130. LAWTON, M. P., and PHILLIPS, R. W. (1956): The relationship between excessive cigarette smoking and psychological tension. Amer. J. med. Sci., **232**, 397.

131. LEESE, W. L. B. (1956): An investigation into bronchitis. Lancet, **ii**, 762.

132. LICKINT, F. (1953): *Atiologie und Prophylaxe des Lungenkrebses,* Dresden. p. 212.

134. LICKINT, F. (1956): Neure Erkenntnisse auf dem Gebiete des Beziehungen zwischen Raucherbronchitis und Bronchialkrebs. Verh. Deut. Ges. inn. Med., **62**, 121.

135. LILIENFELD, A. M. (1959): Emotional and other selected characteristics of cigarette smokers and non-smokers as related to epidemiological studies of lung cancer and other diseases. J. Nat. Cancer Inst. **22**, 259.

136. LILIENFELD, A. M., LEVIN, M. L., and MOORE, G. E. (1956): The association of smoking with cancer of the urinary bladder in humans. A.M.A. Arch. intern. Med., **98**, 129.

137. LINDSEY, A. J. (1961): Chemistry of tobacco smoke. In *Proceedings of Conference on Smoking and Health*. Charles C. Thomas, Illinois. (In the press).
138. LOWE, C. R. (1956): An association between smoking and respiratory tuberculosis. Brit. med. J., ii, 1081.
139. LOWE, C. R. (1959): Effect of mothers' smoking habits on birth weight of their children. Brit. med. J., ii, 673.
140. LOWE, C. R. (1960). Smoking habits related to injury and absenteeism in industry. Brit. J. prev. Soc. Med., 14, 57.

141. McARTHUR, C., WALDRON, E., and DICKINSON, J. (1958): The psychology of smoking. J. abnorm. soc. Psychol., 56, 267.
142. McDEVITT, E., and WRIGHT, I. S. (1955): The Cardiovascular System. In *The Biologic effects of tobacco*. Edited by E. L. Wynder and J. Garland. Little, Brown and Co., Boston.
143. MACKENZIE, C. (1957): *Sublime Tobacco*. Chatto and Windus: London.
144. MATARAZZO, J. D. and SASLOW, G. (1960): Psychological and related characteristics of smokers and non-smokers. Psychol. Bull., 57, 493.
145. MEDICAL RESEARCH COUNCIL (1957): Tobacco smoking and cancer of the lung. Cmd. 8387. H.M.S.O. Brit. med. J., i, 1523.
146. MINISTER OF HEALTH (1954): Smoking and lung cancer. Brit. med. J., i, 465.
147. MINISTER OF HEALTH (1957): Government action on smoking and lung cancer. Brit. med. J., ii, 49.
148. MINISTER OF HEALTH (1961): Propaganda on smoking. Brit. med. J., i, 62. Hansard, 632, 854.
149. MORRIS, J. N. (1961): Personal communication.
150. MORTON, H. J. V. (1944): Tobacco smoking and pulmonary complications after operation. Lancet, i, 368.

151. NADEL, J. A. and COMROE, J. H. (1961): Acute effects of inhalation of cigarette smoke on airway conductance. J. Appl. Physiol., 16, 713.
152. NATIONAL CANCER INSTITUTE OF CANADA (1958): Lung cancer and smoking. Canad. med. Ass. J., 79, 566.
153. NETHERLANDS MINISTRY OF SOCIAL AFFAIRS AND PUBLIC HEALTH (1957): The Hague: Press Notice No. 1233, and Ned. T. Geneesk., 101, 459.

154. OLSEN, H. C., and GILSON, J. C., (1960): Respiratory symptoms, bronchitis and ventilatory capacity in men: an Anglo-Danish comparison with special reference to differences in smoking habits. Brit. med. J., i, 450.
155. OSWALD, N. C., and MEDVEI, V. C. (1955): Chronic bronchitis: the effect of cigarette smoking. Lancet, ii, 843.

156. PACKARD, R. S. (1960): Smoking and the alimentary tract; a review. Gut., i, 171.
157. PAPPENHEIM, E., and STENGEL, E. (1937): Zur Psychopathologie der Rauchgewohnheiten. Wien klin. W'schr., 354.

158. PASSEY, R. D., BERGEL, F., and LEWIS, G. E. (1955): Cigarette smoking and cancer of the lung. Ann. Rep. British Empire Canc. Camp., 33, 59.
159. PASSEY, R. D. (1961): Experimental pathology of tobacco smoke—the lungs. In *Proceedings of Conference on Smoking and Health*. Charles C. Thomas, Illinois. (In the press).
160. PERRIN, M. J., KRUT, L. H., and BRONTE-STEWART, B. (1961): Smoking and food preference. Brit. med. J., i, 387.
161. PHILLIPS, A. M., PHILLIPS, R. W., and THOMPSON, J. L. (1956): Chronic cough: an analysis of etiologic factors in a survey of 1,274 men. Ann. intern. Med. 45, 216.
162. PICKERING, G. W., and SANDERSON, P. H. (1945). Angina pectoris and tobacco. Clin. sci., 5, 275.
163. PROOSDIJ, C. VAN (1960): *Smoking: its influence on the individual and its role in social medicine*. Elsevier Publishing Co., Amsterdam.
164. IBID. p. 227.
165. PROVOST, A. (1959): *Technique du Tabac*. Heliographia. Lausanne. p. 35 and 36.

166. RAASCHOU-NIELSEN, E. (1960): Smoking habits in twins. Danish med. Bull., 7, 82.
167. RAPP, G. W., DUSZA, B. T., and BLANCHET, L. (1959): Absorption and utility of lobeline as a smoking deterrent. Amer. J. med. Sci., 237, 287.
168. REGISTRAR GENERAL (1958): Decennial Supplement. England and Wales 1951. Occupational Mortality Part II, Vol. 1. Commentary. London, H.M.S.O., p. 35.
169. REID, D. D., and FAIRBAIRN, A. S. (1958): The natural history of chronic bronchitis. Lancet, i, 1147.
170. ROTH, G. M. (1960): Summary of recent reports on the biologic effects of cigarette smoking on the cardiovascular system. Circulation, 22, 161.
171. ROTH, G. M., and SHICK, R. M. (1958): Effect of smoking on the cardiovascular system of man. Circulation, 17, 443.
172. ROTH, G. M., and SHICK, R. M. (1960): The effects of smoking on the peripheral circulation. Dis. Chest., 37, 1.

173. SANDERUD, K. (1958): Squamous metaplasia of the respiratory tract epithelium. Acta Path. et Microbiol. Scand., 43, 47.
174. SCHWARTZ, D., and DENOIX, P. F. (1957): L'enquete francaise sur l'etiologie du cancer broncho-pulmonaire. Role du tabac. Sem. Hop. Paris, 33, 3630.
175. SCHWARTZ, D., ANGUERA, G. and LENÈGRE, J. (1961): Tabac et athérosclérose coronarienne. Rev. franc. Êt. clin. biol., 6, 645.
176. SCHWARTZ, D., FLAMANT, R., LELLOUCH, J., and DENOIX, P.F. (1960): Results of a French survey on the role of tobacco, particularly inhalation, in different cancer sites. J. Nat. Cancer Inst., 26, 1085.
177. SERRA, C., and LAMBIASE, M. (1957): E.M.G. and smoking. Changes in muscle action potentials due to smoking. Acta neurol. (Napoli), 12, 494.

178. SILVETTE, H., LARSON, P. S., and HAAG, H. B. (1957): Immunological aspects of tobacco and smoking. Amer. J. med. Sci., **234**, 561.
179. SIMPSON, W. J. (1957): A preliminary report on cigarette smoking and the incidence of prematurity. Amer. J. Obstet. Gynec., **73**, 808.
180. SNEGIREFF, L. S., and LOMBARD, O. M. (1959): Smoking habits of Massachusetts physicians. Five year follow-up study (1954-1959). New Engl. J. Med., **261**, 603.
181. STARCKE, Ä. (1921): Der Kastrations Komplex Internat. J. Psychoanal., Wien, **7**, 9.
182. ŠTICH, Z. (1961): Deputy Minister of Health for Czechoslovakia. Personal Communication.
183. STOCKS, P. (1952): Epidemiology of Cancer of the Lung in England and Wales. Brit. J. Cancer, **6**, 99.
184. STOCKS, P. (1957): Cancer in North Wales and Liverpool Region. Brit. Emp. Cancer Camp., 35th Ann. Rep. Pt. II.
185. STOCKS, P. (1959): Cancer and bronchitis mortality in relation to atmospheric deposit and smoke. Brit. med. J., **i**, 74.
186. STUDY GROUP OF THE PUBLIC HEALTH DEPT., LONDON SCHOOL OF HYGIENE AND TROPICAL MEDICINE (1959): The smoking habits of school children. Brit. J. prev. soc. Med., **13**, 1.

187. THOMAS, C. B. (1960): Characteristics of smokers compared with non-smokers in a population of healthy young adults, including observations on family history, blood pressure, heart rate, body weight, cholesterol and certain psychologic traits. Ann. intern. Med., **53**, 697.
188. THOMAS, C. B., BATEMAN, J. L., LINDBERG, E. F., and BORNHOLD, H. J. (1956): Observations on the individual effects of smoking on the blood pressure, heart rate, stroke volume and cardiac output of healthy young adults. Ann. intern. Med., **44**, 874.
189. TODD, G. F. (1959): Statistics of smoking. Tobacco Manuf. Stand. Comm. Res. Papers, No. 1. 2nd edition.
190. TODD, G. F., MASON, J. I. (1959): Concordance of smoking habits in monozygotic and dizygotic twins. Heredity, **13**, 417.

191. U.S. STUDY GROUP ON SMOKING AND HEALTH (1957): Smoking and health. Science, **125**, 1129.

192. WEBER, J. H. (1957): Arsenic in cigarette tobacco. J. Sci. Food Agric., **8**, 490.
193. WILLIS, R. A. (1961): The incidence and histological types of pulmonary carcinoma with comments on some fallacies and uncertainties. Med. J. Aust., **i**, 433.
194. WILSON, R. H., MEADOR, R. S., JAY, B. E., and HIGGINS, E. (1960): The pulmonary pathologic physiology of persons who smoke cigarettes. New Engl. J. Med., **262**, 956.
195. WOLMAN, W. A. (1953): A study of cigarettes, cigarette smoke and filters. J. Amer. med. Ass., **152**, 917.

196. WORLD HEALTH ORGANISATION (1960): Epidemiology of cancer of the lung. Report of a study group. Wld. Hlth. Org. techn. Rep. Ser., 192.
197. WYNDER, E. L. (1954): Tobacco as a cause of lung cancer, with special reference to infrequency of lung cancer among non-smokers. Penn. med., J., **57**, 1073.
198. WYNDER, E. L. (EDITOR), (1955): *The Biological Effects of Tobacco: with emphasis on the clinical and experimental aspects.* Little, Brown and Co., Boston.
199. WYNDER, E. L. (1959): Laboratory contributions to the tobacco-cancer problem. Brit. med. J., **i**, 317.
200. WYNDER, E. L. (1961): Personal communication.
201. WYNDER, E. L., and BROSS, I. J. (1957): Aetiological factors in mouth cancer. Brit. med. J., **i**, 1137.
202. WYNDER, E. L., BROSS, I. J., and DAY, E. (1956): A study of environmental factors in cancer of the larynx. Cancer, **9**, 86.
203. WYNDER, E. L., BROSS, I. J., and FELDMAN, R. M. (1957): A study of the aetiological factors in cancer of the mouth. Cancer, Phila., **10**, 1300.
204. WYNDER, E. L., GRAHAM, E. A., and CRONINGER, A. B. (1953, 1955 and 1958): Experimental production of carcinoma with cigarette tar. Part I, Cancer Res., **13**, 855; Part II, ibid., **15**, 445; Part V, ibid., **18**, 1263.
205. WYNDER, E. L., and HOFFMAN, N. D. (1960): Some practical aspects of the smoking-cancer problem. New Engl. J. Med., **262**, 540.
206. WYNDER, E. L., LEMON, F. R., and BROSS, I. J. (1959): Cancer and coronary artery disease among seventh-day Adventists. Cancer, **12**, 1016.
207. WYNDER, E. L., LUPBERGER, A., and GRENER, C. (1956): Experimental production of cancer with cigarette tar: strain differences. Brit. J. Cancer, **10**, 507.
208. WYNDER, E. L., and WRIGHT, G. (1957): A study of tobacco carcinogenesis. Part 1, The primary fractions. Cancer, **10**, 255.
209. YERUSHALMY, J. (1961): On the evaluation of epidemiologic evidence. Methodological considerations. In *Proceedings of Conference on Smoking and Health.* Charles C. Thomas, Illinois, (in the press).

210. ZUKEL, W. J., LEWIS, R. H., ENTERLINE, P. E., PAINTER, R. C., RALSTON, L. S., FAWCETT, R. M., MEREDITH, A. P., and PETERSON, B.: A short-term community study of the epidemiology of coronary heart disease. A preliminary report on the North Dakota study. Amer. J. publ. Hlth., **49**, 1630.

211. BENTLEY, H. R. and BURGAN, J. G. (1961): *Cigarette Smoke Condensate: preparation and routine laboratory estimation.* Tobacco Manuf. Stand. Comn. Res. Paper No. 4. 2nd Edition. Table 8.
212. BROWN, K. E. and CAMPBELL, A. H. (1961): Tobacco, alcohol and tuberculosis. Brit. J. Dis. Chest, **55**, 150.
213. READ, J. and SELBY, T. (1961): Tobacco smoking and ventilatory function of the lungs. Brit. med. J., **ii**, 1104.

~ REGAN, T. J., FRANK, M. J., McGINTY, J. F., ZOBL, E., HELLEMS, H. K. and BING, R. J. (1961): Myocardial response to cigarette smoking in normal subjects and patients with coronary disease. Circulation, **23**, 365.
215. TOBACCO MANUFACTURERS' STANDING COMMITTEE (1961): Personal communication. See note in Appendix 2, p. 58.
216. WYNDER, E. L. (1961): Laboratory contributions to the tobacco-cancer problem. Acta. med. Scand., 170, Suppl. 369, p. 63.

References 41, 57, 51 and 196 provide reviews of smoking and lung cancer.

References 120, 163 and 198 provide reviews of the effects of smoking in general.

Printed in the United States of America